The Hulton Getty Picture Collection

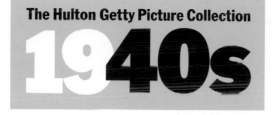

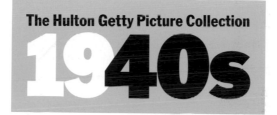

Decades of the 20th Century
Dekaden des 20. Jahrhunderts
Décennies du XX$^e$ siècle

Nick Yapp

KÖNEMANN

First published in 1998 by Könemann Verlagsgesellschaft mbH, Bonner Straße 126, D-50968 Köln

©1998 Könemann Verlagsgesellschaft mbH. Photographs ©1998 Hulton Getty Picture Collection Limited

This book was produced by The Hulton Getty Picture Collection Limited,
Unique House, 21–31 Woodfield Road, London W9 2BA

| For Könemann: | For Hulton Getty: |
|---|---|
| Production director: Detlev Schaper | Art director: Michael Rand |
| Managing editor: Sally Bald | Design: Ian Denning |
| Project editor: Susanne Hergarden | Managing editor: Annabel Else |
| Production assistant: Nicola Leurs | Picture editor: Ali Khoja |
| German translation by: Angela Ritter | Picture research: Alex Linghorn |
| Contributing editor: Daniela Kumor | Editor: James Hughes |
| French translation by: Jean-Luc Lesouëf | Proof reader: Elisabeth Ihre |
| Contributing editor: Michèle Schreyer | Scanning: Paul Wright |
| | Production: Robert Gray |
| | Special thanks: Leon Meyer, |
| | Téa Aganovic and Antonia Hille |

Typesetting by Greiner & Reichel Fotosatz. Colour separation by Jade Reprographics Ltd.
Printed and bound by Sing Cheong Printing Co. Ltd., Hong Kong, China

ISBN 3-8290-0521-0
10  9  8  7  6  5  4

Frontispiece: "When Jenny comes marching home…" The war is over,
and a servicewoman is greeted by her mother and family on her
"demob" from the Women's Auxiliary Air Force. 10 september 1945.

Frontispiz: „Jenny kehrt heim…" Der Krieg ist vorüber, und eine
Militärangehörige wird nach ihrer Entlassung aus der weiblichen
Hilfstruppe der Luftwaffe von ihrer Familie empfangen,
10. September 1945.

Frontispice : « Jenny rentrant chez elle… » La guerre est terminée
et une auxiliaire de l'Armée de l'air est acceuillie par sa mère et sa
famille après sa démobilisation, le 10 septembre 1945.

# Contents / Inhalt / Sommaire

# Introduction

More than any other decade in the century, the 1940s were split down the middle. All was war and destruction until 1945. A good deal was post-war reconstruction thereafter. It was a time when everything was in short supply – except arms and ammunition. For most of the decade, people lived in the dark, deprived of electricity, the truth, food, clothes and any semblance of comfort. In war and peace, they ate what they could get: horse, whale meat, dried egg, ersatz coffee made of acorns, rats and spam.

For five long, desperate years large chunks of the world were battlegrounds – in Europe, North Africa, the Pacific and the Atlantic, Burma, China, the Philippines, and vast swathes of the Soviet Union. People fought for freedom, dug for victory, prayed for liberation. It was an age of heroism and brutality, of triumph and suffering, of bravery and cowardice (not all of it during the war), of determination in the best and worst of causes. And it was a decade that was to produce three almighty hangovers: the Holocaust, the Bomb and the Cold War.

When the fighting at last stopped, whole populations searched and scratched about them – looking for their homes, their families, work, a meaning for life, and a reason for living. For some there was the excitement of being part of a new nation, in Israel, India, Pakistan and Communist China.

By and large, escapism was hard to come by. After the war, the circus came back to town. Sport returned, with record gates at football, cricket and baseball games. Australian cricket maestro Don Bradman bowed out at the Oval. Stanley Matthews, footballing genius, wove his magic at Wembley. Joe Louis floored his opponents wherever he came across them. Gorgeous Gussie Moran brought sex to tennis. The New York Yankees won two of the four post-war baseball World Series.

Fashion had a bumpy ride. Until 1945, it was fashionable to be in uniform. Civilian suits and dresses were subject to restrictions on both the quantity and quality of material used. Clothes, like so many other things were 'rationed'. But when the fighting stopped, along came Christian Dior and others with the New Look, a return to the sumptuous.

There was a whole new glossary of words spawned by the war: 'blitz', 'evacuee', 'GI', 'Home Guard', 'jeep', 'pontoon bridge', 'lend lease'. With the coming of peace, new words emerged: 'prefab', 'demob', 'nylon'. Anne Frank's diary was published. George Orwell wrote *Animal Farm* and *1984*. Bertrand Russell wrote *A History of Western Philosophy*. Gandhi was asked what he thought of Western civilization. 'I think,' he said, 'it would be a very good idea.'

Aviator Amy Johnson and musician Glenn Miller disappeared. Film stars Jane Russell and Frank Sinatra arrived. *Casablanca* became famous as a film. Casablanca became famous as the meeting place of Churchill, Roosevelt and de Gaulle. Four boys stumbled upon the prehistoric painted caves of Lascaux. Hundreds of scientists unlocked the secret of splitting the atom.

And the United Nations brought new hope for the future.

# Einführung

Im Gegensatz zu anderen Dekaden des 20. Jahrhunderts muß man in den vierziger Jahren zwei Phasen unterscheiden: Die Jahre bis 1945 waren von Krieg und Zerstörung geprägt, anschließend erfolgte der Wiederaufbau. Es waren Zeiten, in denen es schier an allem mangelte – außer an Waffen und Munition. Den größten Teil dieses Jahrzehnts lebten die Menschen im wahrsten Sinne des Wortes im Dunkeln; es gab keinen Strom, keine Nahrung, keine Kleidung und nicht den leisesten Hauch von Trost oder Gewißheit. Zu Kriegs- wie zu Friedenszeiten wurde alles verzehrt, was eßbar war: Pferde- und Walfleisch, Trockenei, Ersatzkaffee aus Eicheln, Ratten und Dosenfleisch.

Fünf endlose und hoffnungslose Jahre lang waren große Teile der Erde Schlachtfelder: Europa, Nordafrika, der Pazifische und der Atlantische Ozean, Burma, China, die Philippinen und weite Gebiete der Sowjetunion. Die Menschen kämpften um die Freiheit, schaufelten Schützengräben für den Sieg und sehnten sich nach ihrer Befreiung. Es war eine Zeit der Helden und der Brutalität, des Triumphes und der Niederlage, der Tapferkeit und der Feigheit (die sich nicht auf den Krieg beschränkten), eine Zeit der Entschlossenheit, mit der die edelsten aber auch die übelsten Ziele verfolgt wurden. Und es war ein Jahrzehnt, das eine dreifache Erblast hinterlassen sollte – den Holocaust, die Atombombe und den Kalten Krieg.

Als die Kämpfe schließlich ein Ende fanden, scharrten und suchten die Menschen allerorten in den Trümmern – nach ihren Wohnungen, ihren Familien, nach Arbeit, nach dem Sinn des Lebens und nach etwas, für das es sich zu leben lohnte. Manche hatten teil an der aufregenden Erfahrung, einen neuen Staat zu gründen – so in Israel, Indien, Pakistan und dem kommunistischen China.

Im großen und ganzen war es schwer, der Wirklichkeit zu entkommen. Doch bald schon kehrte das Leben in die Stadt zurück. Es gab wieder Sportveranstaltungen, und die Zuschauerzahlen bei Fußball-, Kricket- und Baseballspielen brachen alle alten Rekordmarken. Das australische Kricket-Genie Don Bradman machte sein letztes Spiel auf dem Londoner Kricket-Feld The Oval. Der Fußballstar Stanley Matthews zauberte im Wembley-Stadion. Der Boxer Joe Louis triumphierte über all seine Gegner. Die hinreißende Gussie Moran machte das Tennisspiel sexy. Und die New York Yankees gewannen im Baseball zwei der vier World-Series-Titel der Nachkriegszeit.

Die Mode fuhr derweil Achterbahn. Bis 1945 trug man Uniform. Anzüge und Kleider für Zivilisten waren nicht nur hinsichtlich der Menge sondern auch der Qualität des verwendeten Stoffes Beschränkungen unterworfen. Kleidung war, wie so viele andere Dinge des täglichen Lebens, streng rationiert. Nach Kriegsende kreierte Christian Dior gemeinsam mit anderen Modeschöpfern den „New Look", die Rückkehr zum luxuriösen und aufwendigen Stil.

Der Krieg hatte viele neue englische Wörter hervorgebracht: „Blitzkrieg", „Evakuierter", „GI", „Bürgerwehr", „Jeep", „Pontonbrücke" und „Leihpacht". Der wiedergewonnene Frieden prägte ebenfalls neue Begriffe: „Fertighaus", „Demobilisierung" und „Nylon". *Das Tagebuch der Anne Frank* wurde veröffentlicht. George Orwell schrieb *Animal Farm* sowie *1984* und Bertrand Russell *A History of Western Philosophy*. Gandhi antwortete folgendermaßen auf die Frage, was er von der westlichen Zivilisation halte: „Ich denke, das wäre eine sehr gute Idee."

Die Fliegerin Amy Johnson und der Musiker Glenn Miller verschwanden von der Bildfläche. Die Filmstars Jane Russell und Frank Sinatra erschienen. Casablanca erlangte Berühmtheit als Film und als Konferenzort von Churchill, Roosevelt und de Gaulle. Vier Kinder entdeckten durch Zufall die prähistorischen Höhlenmalereien von Lascaux, während Hunderte von Wissenschaftlern das Geheimnis der atomaren Kernspaltung lüfteten.

Und die Vereinten Nationen brachten neue Hoffnung für die Zukunft.

# Introduction

Plus que toute autre décennie du siècle, les années quarante se composent de deux pans diamétralement opposés. Jusqu'en 1945, tout a été guerre et destruction. La reconstruction de l'après-guerre qui s'ensuivit a été une œuvre admirable. Ce fut une époque durant laquelle on manquait de tout – excepté d'armes et de munitions. Pendant la majorité de cette décennie, les gens ont vécu dans l'obscurité, sans électricité, sans vérité, vêtements ou tout ce qui aurait ressemblé à du confort. En temps de guerre comme en temps de paix, ils ont mangé ce qu'ils pouvaient se procurer : de la viande de cheval ou de baleine, des œufs desséchés, de l'ersatz de café fait à partir de glands, des rats et de succédant de viande.

Pendant cinq longues et désespérantes années, de vastes régions du monde entier se sont transformées en champs de bataille – en Europe, en Afrique du Nord, dans le Pacifique et l'Atlantique, en Birmanie, en Chine, aux Philippines, ainsi que dans une grande partie de l'Union soviétique. Des peuples se sont battus pour la liberté, ont travaillé pour la victoire, prié pour la libération. Ce fut une époque d'héroïsme et de brutalité, de triomphes et de souffrances, de courage et de couardise (et pas seulement durant la guerre), de détermination pour la meilleure et la pire des causes. Mais ce fut aussi une décennie qui engendra trois faits désormais indélébiles : l'Holocauste, la Bombe et la Guerre froide.

Lorsque les hostilités cessent, des populations entières sont en quête d'elles-mêmes – recherchant leur maison, leur famille, leur travail, un sens à leur vie et une raison de vivre. Pour certains, il y eut l'excitation d'appartenir désormais à une nouvelle nation : Israël, l'Inde, le Pakistan ou la Chine communiste.

Dans l'ensemble, il était difficile de trouver un dérivatif. Après la guerre, la vie reprend ses droits. On s'adonne de nouveau au sport avec des affluences records dans les stades de football, de cricket et de base-ball. Le grand champion australien de cricket Don Bradman tire sa révérence à l'Oval, le célèbre terrain de cricket au sud de Londres. Stanley Matthews, footballeur de génie, fascine les foules à Wembley. Joe Louis écrase les adversaires qui osent le défier. La ravissante Gussie Moran donne une touche de sex-appeal au tennis. Et les New York Yankees gagnent deux des quatre World Series de base-ball de l'après-guerre.

La mode connut une histoire agitée. Jusqu'en 1945, il était de bon ton de porter l'uniforme. Les costumes et vêtements civils faisaient l'objet de restrictions tant pour la quantité que pour la qualité du matériau utilisé. Les vêtements, comme bien d'autres choses encore, étaient « rationnés ». Mais lorsque les hostilités cessèrent, Christian Dior et d'autres firent leur apparition avec le New Look, un retour au somptueux.

Une foule de néologismes naquit durant la guerre : « Blitz », « réfugié », « GI », « Territoriaux », « Jeep », « pont de pontons », « loyer-bail ». Avec l'arrivée de la paix apparaissent aussi des mots nouveaux : « préfabriqué », « démobilisation », « nylon ». Le *Journal d'Anne Frank* est publié. George Orwell écrit *La Ferme des animaux* et *1984*. Bertrand Russel rédige son *Histoire de la philosophie occidentale*. Interrogé sur ce qu'il pense de la civilisation occidentale, Gandhi répond : « Je pense que ce serait une très bonne idée ».

L'aviateur Amy Johnson et le musicien Glenn Miller disparaissent. On assiste en revanche à l'ascension de Jane Russell et Frank Sinatra. *Casablanca* devient un film culte. Et Casablanca devient célèbre comme ville de conférence entre Churchill, Roosevelt et De Gaulle. Quatre gamins découvrent par hasard les peintures rupestres et préhistoriques de Lascaux. Des centaines de scientifiques trouvent le secret de la fission de l'atome.

Et les Nations unies font naître un nouvel espoir pour l'avenir.

# 1. Total war
# Der totale Krieg
# La guerre totale

A US infantryman stands guard over a beachhead on the
Pacific island of Okinawa in 1945. The coral reef in
the background has been dynamited to prepare a landing
place for American supply ships.

Ein Soldat der amerikanischen Infanterie im Jahre 1945
auf Wachposten am Strand der Pazifischen Insel Okinawa.
Das Korallenriff im Hintergrund wurde für einen Anlege-
platz für amerikanische Versorgungsschiffe gesprengt.

Un fantassin américain monte la garde en haut d'une
plage de l'île d'Okinawa, dans le Pacifique, en 1945.
Le récif de corail à l'arrière-plan vient d'être dynamité
pour que les péniches de débarquement américaines
puissent atteindre la plage.

# 1. Total war
# Der totale Krieg
# La guerre totale

When Churchill growled of fighting on the seas and oceans, on the beaches, on the landing grounds, in the fields, in the streets, and in the hills, he knew what he was talking about, though it didn't all come to pass in Britain.

World War II savaged people's lives in a way no other had. The Soviet Union suffered most in terms of casualties. Germany and Japan suffered most in terms of destruction and the misery of defeat. If ever proof was needed of the waste and stupidity of war in general, this war specifically provided it.

And yet few doubted that it had to be fought, and with every weapon available. The stakes were high. On the one side was a Reich boasting it would last 1,000 years. On the other, old empires and new democracies somehow glued together.

Graveyards sprang up all over the world: in the Pacific, the Atlantic, North Africa, the whole of Europe, the Far East, even in a South American river mouth. You could be killed thousands of miles from home or in your own backyard. Death came hurtling from the clouds, slinking from under the sea, and scorching across the earth. In all, some 50 million people were killed in the war.

Als Churchill bedrückt verkündete, es werde Krieg auf allen Weltmeeren, an den Küsten, in den Häfen und auf dem Land, in den Straßen und in den Bergen geben, wußte er, wovon er sprach. Allerdings sollte sich nicht alles in Großbritannien abspielen.

Der Zweite Weltkrieg war so brutal und schonungslos wie kein anderer Krieg zuvor. Die Sowjetunion verzeichnete die höchste Zahl an Todesopfern; Deutschland und Japan waren größtenteils zerstört und mußten mit dem Elend der Niederlage fertigwerden. Wenn es je eines Beweises dafür bedurfte, daß Krieg eine besonders perfide Form der Verschwendung und

Dummheit ist, so verdeutlicht dies insbesondere dieser Krieg. Und dennoch hatte kaum jemand die Notwendigkeit bezweifelt, daß man diese Auseinandersetzung mit jeder zur Verfügung stehenden Waffe führen mußte. Es stand eine Menge auf dem Spiel. Auf der einen Seite ein Reich, das damit prahlte, 1000 Jahre zu überdauern. Auf der anderen Seite ein Verbund alter Imperien und junger Demokratien.

Überall auf der Welt entstanden Friedhöfe: im Pazifischen Ozean, im Atlantik, in Nordafrika, in ganz Europa, im Fernen Osten, sogar im Mündungsgebiet eines südamerikanischen Flusses. Man konnte Tausende Kilometer von der Heimat entfernt getötet werden oder aber vor der eigenen Haustür. Der Tod kam vom Himmel herunter, schlich sich aus den Tiefen des Meeres heran und raste über die Erde. Insgesamt kamen in diesem Krieg 50 Millionen Menschen ums Leben.


Lorsque Churchill fait sa proclamation de la lutte sur les mers et les océans, sur les plages, sur les aéroports, dans les champs, dans les rues et dans les collines, il sait ce dont il parle, bien que tout ne se soit pas passé en Grande-Bretagne.

La Seconde Guerre mondiale ravagea la vie des gens comme ne le fit aucune autre guerre auparavant. C'est l'Union soviétique qui subit les plus lourdes pertes en termes de vies humaines. L'Allemagne et le Japon, en termes de destruction, de misère et de défaite. S'il avait jamais été besoin de prouver l'inanité et la stupidité de la guerre en général, cette guerre l'aura prouvé sans appel.

Et, pourtant, peu avaient mis en doute la nécessité de se battre, avec toutes les armes possibles. L'enjeu était élevé. D'un côté, il y avait un Reich se vantant de durer mille ans. De l'autre, de vieux empires et de nouvelles démocraties qui s'allièrent par la force des choses.

Les cimetières se multiplièrent dans le monde entier : dans le Pacifique, dans l'Atlantique, en Afrique du Nord, dans l'Europe entière, à l'Extrême-Orient, et même dans l'estuaire d'un fleuve d'Amérique du Sud. Vous pouviez aussi bien être tué à des milliers de kilomètres de chez vous que dans votre propre jardin. La mort frappait en s'abattant de derrière les nuages, en se glissant furtivement sous la mer et en déferlant sur la terre. Au total, la guerre a fait quelque 50 millions de victimes.

Hitler and Marshal of the Reich Hermann Goering take time out from the disasters of 1942. Two years later Goering was in disgrace.

Hitler und Reichsmarschall Hermann Göring entspannen sich nach den Katastrophen von 1942. Zwei Jahre später fiel Göring in Ungnade.

Hitler et le Reichsmarschall Hermann Goering se reposent des catastrophes de 1942. Deux ans plus tard, Goering tombait en disgrâce.

A Cherbourg docker lights Churchill's cigar. Churchill was visiting what was left of the French port in June 1944, just a few days after the D day landings. The town suffered a week-long siege before it was liberated.

Ein Dockarbeiter in Cherbourg gibt Churchill Feuer für seine Zigarre. Der britische Premierminister besuchte die Überreste des französischen Hafens im Juni 1944, nur wenige Tage nach der Landung der alliierten Truppen am Tag X. Nach einer Woche Belagerung konnte die Stadt befreit werden.

Un docker de Cherbourg allume le cigare de Churchill rendant visite à ceux qui avaient survécu dans le port français, en juin 1944, quelques jours après le Jour J. Avant d'être libérée, la ville avait été assiégée pendant une semaine.

Disaster at Dieppe. Canadian survivors of an ill-planned attack on Dieppe return to Britain, August 1942. They lost half their comrades. The raid was an ill-conceived rehearsal for D-day two years later.

Fiasko bei Dieppe. Kanadier, die einen schlecht geplanten Angriff auf Dieppe überlebten, kehren im August 1942 nach Großbritannien zurück. Sie verloren die Hälfte ihrer Kameraden bei dieser verunglückten Offensive für den Tag X, der zwei Jahre später ein Erfolg werden sollte.

Désastre à Dieppe. Des Canadiens survivants d'une attaque mal préparée contre Dieppe rentrent en Grande-Bretagne, en août 1942. Ils ont perdu la moitié de leurs camarades. Le raid était une répétition générale mal préparée du Jour J, deux ans plus tard.

Disaster at Dunkirk. The French destroyer *Bourrasque* sinks off the Dunkirk beaches during the withdrawal of Allied troops. While they were being loaded with their human cargo, ships like these were sitting targets for German planes.

Fiasko bei Dünkirchen. Der französische Zerstörer *Bourrasque* sinkt vor der Küste bei Dünkirchen während des Rückzugs der Alliierten. Während die Soldaten an Bord gingen, waren solche Schiffe eine leichte Beute für deutsche Kriegsflugzeuge.

Désastre à Dunkerque. Le destroyer français *Bourrasque* coule au large des plages de Dunkerque pendant la retraite des troupes alliées. Pendant qu'ils prenaient à leur bord leur cargaison humaine, des bâtiments comme celui-ci étaient à la merci des avions allemands.

Free French. In June 1940, General Charles de Gaulle delivers the speech in which he called on his countrymen and women to continue the fight against Germany, even though France had fallen, and he was himself in exile.

Freie Franzosen. Im Juni 1940 rief General Charles de Gaulle seine Landsleute dazu auf, den Kampf gegen Deutschland weiterzuführen, obwohl Frankreich besiegt war und er selbst sich im Exil befand.

Libérer la France. En juin 1940, le général Charles de Gaulle prononce son célèbre discours où il exhorte ses compatriotes hommes et femmes à poursuivre la lutte contre l'Allemagne même si la France est tombée et lui-même en exil.

Vichy French. Premier Pierre Laval (right) and Marshal Henri Philippe Pétain in 1940. In their collaborationist France, 'Liberty, Equality, Fraternity' was replaced by 'Work, Family and Fatherland'.

Vichy Franzosen. Staatsoberhaupt Pierre Laval (rechts) und Marschall Henri Philippe Pétain im Jahre 1940. In ihrem Frankreich der Kollaboration wurde „Freiheit, Gleichheit, Brüderlichkeit" ersetzt durch „Arbeit, Familie und Vaterland".

Vichy. Le Premier ministre Pierre Laval (à droite) et le maréchal Henri Philippe Pétain, en 1940. Dans leur France de collaborateurs, « Liberté, égalité, fraternité » fit place à « Travail, famille, patrie ».

RAF pilots run to their planes on an alert at a Fleet Air Arm
Training Centre. The Battle of Britain was already over when
this picture was taken in 1943, but the 'scramble' went on.

Piloten der Royal Air Force laufen zu ihren Flugzeugen
bei einem Alarm in einem Trainingszentrum der Luftwaffe.
Als diese Aufnahme 1943 gemacht wurde, war die große
Schlacht um England bereits vorbei. Das Proben von
Soforteinsätzen ging jedoch weiter.

Pilotes de la RAF courant vers leurs avìons lors d'une alerte
dans un camp d'entraînement de l'armée de l'air. La bataille
d'Angleterre était déjà terminée lorsque cette photo fut prise
en 1943, mais l'entraînement de choc continuait.

A lull in the fighting, a battle of wits. RAF pilots relax during the Battle of Britain in March 1940. The jacket and boots worn by the officer on the left suggests they were expecting an 'alert' at any moment.

Eine Pause im Luftkampf für einen Kampf des Geistes. Piloten der Royal Air Force versuchen, sich während der Schlacht um England im März 1940 zu entspannen. Jacke und Stiefel des Offiziers zur Linken lassen darauf schließen, daß man jeden Augenblick mit einem Alarm rechnete.

Le calme avant la tempête : jouer au plus fin. Pilotes de la RAF se reposant durant la bataille d'Angleterre, en mars 1940. Le blouson et les bottes que porte l'officier de gauche indiquent qu'une alerte peut survenir à tout moment.

Easter 1940. British troops sample the delights of NAAFI hot cross buns. To some the Navy Army and Air Force Institutes was a godsend. To others it was a joke: NAAFI tea was even rumoured to lower a man's sex drive.

Ostern 1940. Britische Soldaten testen die Gaumenfreuden der NAAFI-Osterbrötchen. Für manche waren die Navy, Army and Air Force Institutes ein Geschenk Gottes, für andere lediglich ein Witz: Man munkelte sogar, daß NAAFI-Tee dem männlichen Geschlechtstrieb schade.

Pâques 1940. Des soldats britanniques goûtent les délicieux petits pains au lait légèrement épicés du NAAFI. Pour certains, le Navy Army and Air Force Institutes était une bénédiction. Pour d'autres, c'était une plaisanterie : le thé du NAAFI était réputé pour affaiblir les pulsions sexuelles des hommes.

October 1940. At the height of the Battle of Britain, a coastal defence soldier primes Mills bombs. The German invasion was expected at any time.

Oktober 1940. Ein Soldat der Küstenverteidigung beim Scharfmachen von Mills-Bomben im Sturm der Schlacht um England. Die deutsche Invasion konnte jederzeit hereinbrechen.

Octobre 1940. À l'apogée de la bataille d'Angleterre, un soldat de la défense côtière prepare des grenades. On s'attendait à une invasion des Allemands à tout moment.

Advancing to victory. Russian troops in Berlin, April 1945.
The war was almost over. One prominent Nazi, Albert Speer,
reckoned that was a good thing. 'It was just an opera,'
he said. For most Germans, this was *Götterdämmerung*.

Vorstoß zum Sieg. Russische Soldaten in Berlin im April
1945. Der Krieg war fast vorüber, und dies war in den
Augen des prominenten Nazis, Albert Speer, eine gute Sache.
Er hielt den Krieg für eine „Oper". Für die meisten
Deutschen war es die *Götterdämmerung*.

En route vers la victoire. Troupes russes à Berlin en avril
1945. La guerre était presque terminée. Un célèbre nazi,
Albert Speer, admit que c'était une bonne chose. « Ce fut
juste un opéra », dit-il. Pour la majorité des Allemands, ce fut
*Götterdämmerung*.

Advancing to defeat. Exhausted German troops take a break
on their push to Moscow, August 1941. They had just
reached the town of Vitebsk, to find it deserted and ablaze
– a scene they would find repeated in most Russian towns.

Vorstoß zur Niederlage. Erschöpfte deutsche Soldaten
unterbrechen ihren Marsch auf Moskau im August 1941.
Sie hatten soeben die Stadt Witebsk erreicht, die sie
verlassen und in Flammen vorfanden – ein Anblick, der sich
in den meisten russischen Städten wiederholen sollte.

En marche vers la défaite. Des soldats allemands, épuisés,
font une pause durant leur offensive vers Moscou, en août
1941. Ils viennent d'atteindre la ville de Vitebsk, qu'ils
ont trouvée désertée et incendiée – une scène qui devait se
renouveler dans la plupart des villes russes.

Frozen members of the German Wehrmacht on the
Eastern Front, 1942. Tens of thousands died of cold.
Food was scarce. Morale reached rock bottom. Within
a couple of months, the Wehrmacht was in retreat.

Vereiste Angehörige der deutschen Wehrmacht an der
Ostfront, 1942. Zehntausende von Soldaten starben
an der unbarmherzigen Kälte. Die Lebensmittel waren
knapp und die Moral sank auf den Nullpunkt. Nach
einigen Monaten trat die Wehrmacht den Rückzug an.

Soldats gelés de la Wehrmacht allemande sur le front
Est, en 1942. Des dizaines de milliers d'hommes
périrent de froid. La nourriture se faisait rare. Le
moral était au plus bas. Quelques mois plus tard, la
Wehrmacht dut battre en retraite.

The 'Great Patriotic War', 1941. A wounded Russian officer urges his men forward. Losses and suffering on the Soviet side were appalling.

Der „Große patriotische Krieg" von 1941. Ein verwundeter russischer Offizier feuert seine Männer an, weiter vorzudringen. Die Verluste und das Leiden auf sowjetischer Seite nahmen entsetzliche Ausmaße an.

La « Grande guerre patriotique » de 1941. Un officier russe ordonne à ses hommes de poursuivre leur avancée. Les pertes et les souffrances parmi les Soviétiques furent épouvantables.

'A day which will live in infamy.' Explosions shatter
the Naval Air Station at Pearl Harbor on 7 December
1941. 'America was suddenly and deliberately attacked
by the Empire of Japan,' said Roosevelt.
'We will gain the inevitable triumph, so help us God.'

„Ein Tag, der immer an die Schande erinnern wird."
Bombardierungen erschüttern am 7. Dezember 1941
den Marinestützpunkt Pearl Harbor. „Amerika wurde
unvermittelt und vorsätzlich vom Kaiserreich Japan
angegriffen", sagte Roosevelt. „Wir werden den
unabwendbaren Sieg erringen, so wahr uns Gott helfe."

« Un jour qui entrera dans l'histoire comme jour
d'infamie ». Des explosions ébranlent la base aérienne
de Pearl Harbor, le 7 décembre 1941. « L'Amérique a
été attaquée sans préavis et délibérément par l'empire
du Japon », déclara Roosevelt. « Nous allons remporter
un triomphe inévitable, que Dieu nous aide. »

Nearing the end in the West. An exhausted German trooper in Belgium, some months after the D-day landings.

Das nahende Ende im Westen. Ein erschöpfter deutscher Soldat in Belgien, einige Monate nach der Landung der Alliierten am Tag X.

La fin est proche à l'Ouest. Un soldat allemand épuisé en Belgique, quelques mois après le Jour J.

First strike in the
East. A Japanese
pilot completes his
ceremonial dress
before setting out to
bomb Pearl Harbor.

Der erste Schlag im
Osten. Ein japani-
scher Soldat vervoll-
ständigt seine zere-
monielle Bekleidung,
bevor er abfliegt,
um Pearl Harbor
zu bombardieren.

Première offensive
à l'Est. Un pilote
japonais complète
sa tenue rituelle
avant de décoller
pour bombarder
Pearl Harbor.

October 1942.
The first black
servicewomen from
the United States
arrive in Britain.
About half a million
blacks served
overseas in
segregated units.

Oktober 1942. Die
ersten schwarzen
weiblichen
Militärangehörigen
der Vereinigten
Staaten kommen in
Großbritannien an.
Etwa eine halbe
Million Schwarze
diente in Übersee in
Einheiten mit
Rassentrennung.

Octobre 1942.
Les premières
femmes militaires
noires des Etats-Unis
arrivent en Grande-
Bretagne. Plus d'un
demi-million de
noirs ont servi
outre-mer dans des
unités où régnait la
ségrégation raciale.

September 1942. Corporal Raymond Du Pont plays a
hymn on a portable harmonium somewhere in Britain.
Although discrimination persisted in the US Army, black
troops were given a warm welcome by local civilians.

September 1942. Stabsunteroffizier Raymond Du Pont
spielt irgendwo in Großbritannien ein Kirchenlied auf
einem tragbaren Harmonium. Trotz der Rassendis-
kriminierung in der amerikanischen Armee empfingen
die Briten die schwarzen Soldaten herzlich.

Septembre 1942. Le caporal Raymond Du Pont joue un
hymne sur un harmonium portable, quelque part en
Grande Bretagne. Tandis que la discrimination persistait
dans l'armée américaine, les troupes noires furent
accueillies chaleureusement.

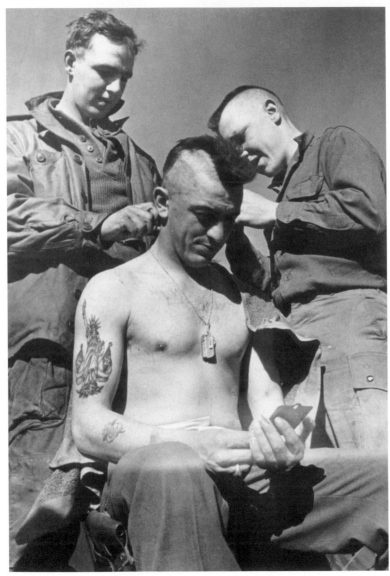

Heads… US paratroopers get a 'Comanche' haircut in March 1945. The next day, they parachuted down six miles east of the Rhine.

Köpfe… Amerikanische Fallschirmjäger erhalten im März 1945 einen Irokesen-Haarschnitt. Am nächsten Tag sprangen sie 10 Kilometer östlich des Rheins in die Tiefe.

De la tête… Des parachutistes américains se font couper les cheveux à l'Iroquois, en mars 1945. Le lendemain, ils vont être parachutés à une dizaine de kilomètres à l'est du Rhin.

Toes... Regular foot inspection was essential for British soldiers of the 7th Armoured Division (the Desert Rats) as they fought their way across North Africa.

Zehen... Regelmäßige Fußinspektionen waren für die britischen Soldaten der 7. Panzerdivision (die Wüstenratten) außerst wichtig, während sie sich quer durch Nordafrika kämpften.

... aux pieds ! Une inspection régulière des pieds était essentielle pour les soldats britanniques de la 7ᵉ Division de blindés (les Rats du désert) durant leur offensive en Afrique du Nord.

A US Liberator
bomber drops
its load on Ploiesti in
1944. Ploiesti was
in the heart of the
Romanian oil fields,
Hitler's major source
of supply.

Ein amerikanischer
Bomber wirft im
Jahre 1944 seine
Bomben über
Ploiesti ab. Ploiesti
lag im Zentrum der
rumänischen
Ölfelder, die Hitlers
wichtigste Versor-
gungsquelle waren.

Un Liberator
américain largue ses
bombes sur Ploiesti
en 1944. Au cœur
des gisements de
pétrole roumains,
Ploiesti était la
principale source
d'approvisionnement
de Hitler.

500-pound bombs from a Flying Fortress hurtle toward the oil refinery at Livorno (Leghorn), Italy, towards the end of the war.

Von einer Flying Fortress abgeworfene 500-Pfund-Bomben fallen gegen Kriegsende auf die Ölraffinerie im italienischen Livorno.

Des bombes de 500 livres larguées par une Forteresse volante tombent droit sur la raffinerie de pétrole de Livourne, en Italie, vers la fin de la guerre.

Jewish deportees arriving at Auschwitz, Poland, in 1940.
Of all the infamous concentration camps, Auschwitz was
perhaps the worst. It is unlikely that any of the people in
this photograph survived the war.

Deportierte Juden bei ihrer Ankunft im polnischen
Auschwitz, 1940. Von allen Konzentrationslagern war
Auschwitz wohl das schlimmste. Es ist unwahrscheinlich,
daß eine der abgebildeten Personen den Krieg überlebte.

Déportés juifs arrivant à Auschwitz, en Pologne, en 1940.
De tous les terribles camps de concentration, Auschwitz a
peut-être été le pire. Il est fort probable qu'aucun des
hommes visibles sur cette photo n'a survécu aux horreurs
de la guerre.

German civilian prisoners captured by Polish patriots in Warsaw, August 1944. The Poles rose against German occupying troops, believing that the Russians were only a few days' fighting away. But no help came, and the rising was brutally crushed.

Deutsche Zivilisten, die im August 1944 von polnischen Patrioten in Warschau gefangengenommen wurden. Die Polen erhoben sich gegen die deutschen Besatzungstruppen in dem Glauben, daß die Russen sich innerhalb weniger Tage zu ihnen durchkämpfen würden. Die Hilfe blieb jedoch aus, und der Aufstand wurde brutal niedergeschlagen.

Civils allemands faits prisonniers par les patriotes polonais à Varsovie, en août 1944. Les Polonais se soulevèrent contre les troupes d'occupation allemandes, croyant que les Russes n'étaient plus qu'à quelques jours de combat. Mais personne ne leur vint en aide et leur soulèvement fut noyé dans le sang.

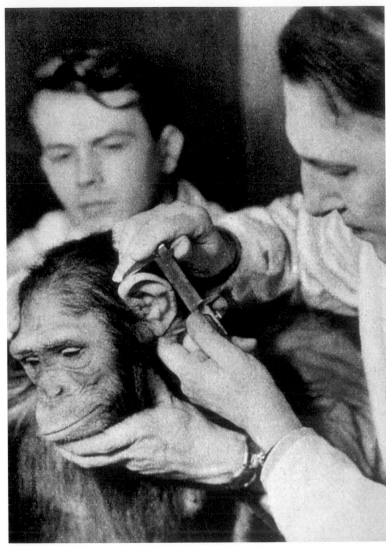

German zoologists chart the process of evolution, 1940. The ape will be better treated than millions of human beings.

Deutsche Zoologen untersuchen den Prozeß der Evolution, 1940. Dieser Affe wird besser behandelt werden als Millionen von Menschen.

Des zoologistes allemands étudient le processus évolutionniste, en 1940. Le singe sera mieux traité que des millions d'êtres humains.

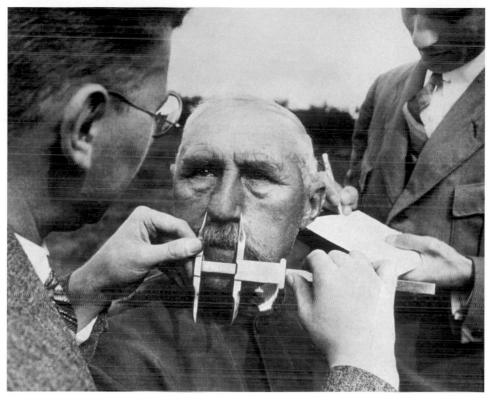

At the height of Nazi persecution of the Jews, an old man's physiognomy is measured by investigators. In some cases the fate of a subject depended on the measurements of his or her features.

Auf dem Höhepunkt der Judenverfolgung mißt ein Untersuchungsbeamter die Physiognomie eines alten Mannes. Das Schicksal des Untersuchten hing von den Maßen seiner Gesichtszüge ab.

Au plus fort des persécutions des juifs par les nazis, des inspecteurs étudient la physionomie d'un vieil homme. Dans certains cas, le destin de la personne dépendait de la forme de son crâne.

Jewish civilians from the Warsaw ghetto surrender to German soldiers in 1943. Of the 600,000 Jews who were confined there, only 60,000 survived – among them the young boy in the foreground of this picture. Most of the others perished in the death camps.

Jüdische Zivilisten aus dem Warschauer Ghetto ergeben sich deutschen Soldaten im Jahre 1943. Von den 600.000 Juden, die dort eingesperrt waren, überlebten nur 60.000 – unter ihnen der Junge im Vordergrund dieser Aufnahme. Die meisten anderen kamen in Konzentrationslagern um.

Civils juifs du ghetto de Varsovie se rendant aux soldats allemands en 1943. Des 600 000 juifs enfermés ici, seuls 60 000 survécurent – parmi eux, le jeune garçon au premier plan sur la photo. La plupart des autres périrent dans les camps de la mort.

The battle for Stalingrad, 1943. Soviet troops defend the ruins of the Red October plant in some of the bitterest fighting of the war.

Der Kampf um Stalingrad, 1943. Sowjetische Soldaten verteidigen die Ruine der Werft Roter Oktober in einem der erbittertsten Kämpfe des Krieges.

Bataille de Stalingrad, 1943. Des soldats soviétiques défendent les ruines de l'usine Octobre rouge lors de l'un des affrontements les plus terribles de la guerre.

The battle of Kursk, 1943 A German artilleryman sits on the remains of his gun, a dead comrade by his side.

Der Kampf um Kursk, 1943. Ein deutscher Artillerist sitzt auf den Überresten seines Geschützes, einen toten Kameraden an seiner Seite.

Bataille de Kursk, 1943. Un artilleur allemand est assis sur ce qui reste de son canon, un camarade gît mort à ses côtés.

The last few minutes before 'hitting the beach'. American soldiers shelter in their landing craft early in the war. It was a scene repeated a thousand times all over the world, from Europe to North Africa to the Pacific Islands.

Die letzten Minuten vor dem „Strandangriff". Zu Beginn des Krieges suchen amerikanische Soldaten Schutz in ihrem Landungsboot. Diese Szene wiederholte sich tausendfach überall auf der Welt, von Europa über Nordafrika bis zu den Pazifischen Inseln.

Les ultimes minutes avant d'atteindre la plage. Des soldats américains s'abritent dans leur péniche de débarquement, au début de la guerre. Cette scène allait se répéter des milliers de fois dans le monde entier, de l'Europe à l'Afrique du Nord et aux îles du Pacifique.

The soft underbelly of the Nazi empire. Allied troops commanded by General Patton wade ashore during the invasion of Sicily in July 1943. Eisenhower called it 'the first page in the liberation of the European continent'.

Die Achillesferse des Nazireichs. Von General Patton befehligte alliierte Truppen waten an Land während der Invasion Siziliens im Juli 1943. Eisenhower nannte die Landung auf Sizilien „die erste Etappe der Befreiung des europäischen Kontinents".

Le talon d'Achille des nazis. Troupes alliées commandées par le général Patton arrivant sur une plage durant le débarquement de Sicile, en juillet 1943. Eisenhower le qualifia de « première étape de la libération du continent européen ».

Striking inland. Just a couple of miles from Utah
Beach in Normandy, American soldiers of the US 4th
Army rain shells on retreating German soldiers in
the little town of Carentan. Great battles lay ahead.

Angriff im Landesinneren. Nur wenige Kilometer
von Utah Beach in der Normandie entfernt lassen
amerikanische Soldaten der 4. US-Armee in der
kleinen Stadt Carentan einen Granathagel auf sich
zurückziehende deutsche Soldaten niedergehen.
Die großen Schlachten liegen noch vor ihnen.

Attaque derrière la ligne de front. A quelques
kilomètres de Utah Beach, en Normandie, des
soldats de la 4ᵉ armée américaine font pleuvoir des
bombes sur des soldats allemands qui se replient,
dans la petite ville de Carentan. Mais les grandes
batailles étaient encore à venir.

Russian infantrymen
fight their way street
by street through
the suburbs of
Berlin, May 1945.
The Reich was in its
death throes.

Russische Infanteri-
sten erkämpfen sich
Straße für Straße
ihren Weg durch die
Außenbezirke Berlins
im Mai 1945. Das
Deutsche Reich
lag in den letzten
Zügen.

Fantassins russes
progressant rue
après rue dans la
banlieue de Berlin,
en mai 1945. Le
Reich est à l'agonie.

November 1944.
US Army Captain
Tom Carothers and
Lieutenant Roy
Green display the
'liberated' jacket of a
German general.

November 1944.
Hauptmann Tom
Carothers und
Leutnant Roy Green
der amerikanischen
Armee stellen die
„befreite" Jacke
eines deutschen
Generals zur Schau.

Novembre 1944.
Le capitaine de
l'armée américaine
Tom Carothers et
le lieutenant Roy
Green présentent la
veste « libérée » d'un
général allemand.

The aftermath of war. Cologne Cathedral stands above the ruins of a great
city. In the foreground is the twisted metal of the Hohenzollernbrücke.
The picture was taken in 1946, a year after the war ended.

Die Auswirkungen des Krieges. Der Kölner Dom überragt die Ruinen einer
großartigen Stadt. Im Vordergrund der verbogene Stahl der Hohenzollernbrücke. Die Aufnahme entstand 1946, ein Jahr nach Kriegsende.

Les séquelles de la guerre. La cathédrale de Cologne domine les ruines de
la grande ville. Au premier plan, les vestiges effondrés du pont
Hohenzollern. Le cliché a été pris en 1946, un an après la fin de la guerre.

British, Russian and
American troops on
the balcony of the
Chancellery in Berlin
celebrate the death
of Hitler.

Britische, russische
und amerikanische
Soldaten feiern auf
dem Balkon der
Berliner Reichskanz-
lei den Tod Hitlers.

Soldats britanniques,
russes et américains
sur le balcon de la
Chancellerie du
Reich, à Berlin,
célébrant la mort de
Hitler.

April 1944. US troops on the Pacific island of Bougainville prepare for a reconnaissance mission. As the Americans advanced through the North Solomon Islands, they frequently left behind them Japanese pockets of resistance that had to be cleared by following troops.

April 1944. US-Soldaten bereiten sich auf der Pazifischen Insel Bougainville auf einen Aufklärungseinsatz vor. Während ihres Vorstoßes durch die nördlichen Salomonen ließen die Amerikaner häufig Widerstandsnester der Japaner zurück, die nachrückende Einheiten beseitigen mußten.

Avril 1944. Troupes américaines sur l'île de Bougainville, dans le Pacifique, se préparant pour une mission de reconnaissance. Lors de leur progression vers le nord des îles Salomon, les Américains laissèrent fréquemment derrière eux des poches de résistance japonaises que les troupes qui suivaient se devaient d'éliminer.

A good year for the General. President Roosevelt (right) and Douglas MacArthur (far left) celebrate MacArthur's appointment as Chief of Staff of the US Army, 1944. In that year, MacArthur led the advance through the Pacific Islands, returned to the Philippines and was promoted to five-star general.

Ein gutes Jahr für den General. Präsident Roosevelt (rechts) feiert 1944 mit Douglas MacArthur (ganz links) dessen Ernennung zum Stabschef der Armee der Vereinigten Staaten. In jenem Jahr befehligte MacArthur den Vorstoß durch die Pazifischen Inseln, kehrte zu den Philippinen zurück und wurde zum Fünf-Sterne-General befördert.

Une bonne année pour le général. Le président Roosevelt (à droite) et Douglas MacArthur (à l'extrême gauche) célèbrent la promotion de MacArthur comme chef de l'état-major de l'armée américaine, en 1944. Cette année-là, MacArthur dirigea l'offensive à travers les îles du Pacifique, revint aux Philippines et fut promu général cinq étoiles.

Two minds with but a single thought: 'Who gets the bigger influence over
Europe when the fighting stops?' Allied leaders Stalin and Churchill in a rare
moment of joviality at the Yalta (Ukraine) Conference in February 1945.

Zwei Köpfe, ein Gedanke: „Wer wird den größeren Einfluß auf Europa
haben, wenn der Krieg vorüber ist?" Stalin und Churchill in einem seltenen
Augenblick der Heiterkeit auf der Konferenz von Jalta (Ukraine) im
Februar 1945.

Deux esprits, mais une seule pensée : « Qui exercera la plus grande influence
sur l'Europe après la fin des hostilités ? » Les leaders alliés, Staline et
Churchill, lors d'un rare moment de détente durant la conférence de Yalta,
en Ukraine, en février 1945.

Defeat for Germany. General Alfred Jodl (centre) signs the German
surrender at Allied commander Eisenhower's headquarters in
Reims on 7 May 1945. On the left is Major Wilhelm Orenius, on
the right Admiral of the Fleet Georg von Friedeburg.

Niederlage für Deutschland. In Reims im Hauptquartier des
Befehlshabers der Alliierten, Eisenhower, unterzeichnet
Generaloberst Alfred Jodl (Mitte) die deutsche Kapitulation
am 7. Mai 1945. Zu seiner Rechten Major Wilhelm Orenius,
zur Linken Großadmiral Georg von Friedeburg.

Défaite pour l'Allemagne. Le général Alfred Jodl (au centre) signe
l'acte de reddition allemand au quartier général allié d'Eisenhower,
à Reims, le 7 mai 1945. A gauche, le major Wilhelm Orenius ;
à droite, l'amiral de la flotte Georg von Friedeburg.

Defeat for Japan. The Japanese Foreign Minister, Mamoro Shigemitsu, discusses surrender terms with Lieutenant General Richard Sutherland on board the USS *Missouri*.

Niederlage für Japan. Der japanische Außenminister, Mamoro Shigemitsu, diskutiert die Bedingungen der Kapitulation mit Generalleutnant Richard Sutherland an Bord der USS *Missouri*.

Défaite pour le Japon. Le ministre japonais des Affaires étrangères, Mamoro Shigemitsu, discute les termes de la reddition avec le lieutenant-général Richard Sutherland à bord du USS *Missouri*.

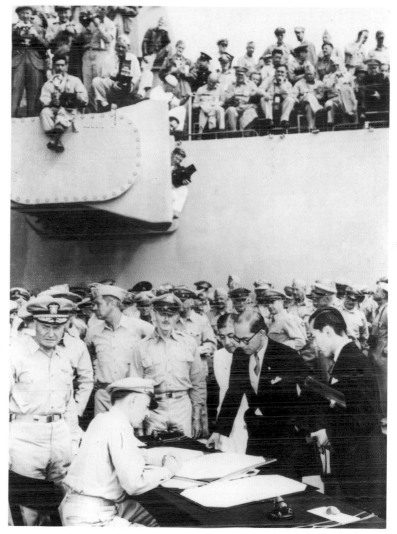

# 2. The home front
## Die Heimatfront
## Le front à domicile

'London can take it.' At the height of the Blitz, a London family emerges from the ruins of their house with the prized possessions that they have salvaged, including grandma's potted plant.

„London wird damit fertig." Als sich der deutsche Luftangriff auf britische Städte (Blitz) auf dem Höhepunkt befindet, trägt eine Londoner Familie aus den Trümmern ihres Hauses die wertvollsten Stücke, die gerettet werden konnten, einschließlich Großmutters Topfpflanze.

« Londres ne se laissera pas abattre. » A l'apogée du Blitz, une famille londonienne émerge des ruines de sa maison, portant dignement tout ce qu'elle a pu sauver, y compris la plante verte de la grand-mère.

# 2. The home front
# Die Heimatfront
# Le front à domicile

It was the citizens' war. Heinkels, Halifaxes and Flying Fortresses brought the horrors of war to suburban streets and city centres. No one was safe. The shelter in the back garden or the platform of a tube station were constant reminders that everyone was involved in the fighting.

There were ration books and queues for food. When a few extra onions were available, word spread quickly, and butchers and greengrocers had a hard time convincing all of their even-handedness. There was the blackout: a mere chink of light brought the fury of an air raid warden down upon a house – but that was better than a bomb.

Children were sent away from the cities to the comparative safety of the country. Some enjoyed the change. Some hated it. A few walked doggedly back home. It depended on the child and the sort of welcome they received.

Old men and boys dressed in uniforms and guarded crossroads, coastlines, railway tunnels. Everyone was told to guard their tongues: 'Careless talk costs lives;' 'Be like Dad, keep Mum.'

Somehow civilization survived. And before the 1940s were over, there were even some who looked back on the war years with a fond nostalgia.


Es war der Krieg der Zivilisten. Flugzeuge des Typs Heinkel, Halifax und Flying Fortress brachten den Kriegsschrecken in die Vororte und die Stadtzentren. Niemand konnte sich sicher fühlen. Der Bunker im Garten oder der Bahnsteig einer U-Bahn-Station erinnerten ständig daran, daß jedermann von diesem Krieg betroffen war.

Es gab Bezugsscheine und Warteschlangen für Lebensmittel. Waren einmal ein paar Zwiebeln mehr zu haben, verbreitete sich die Nachricht in Windeseile, und die Gemüsehändler hatten Mühe, alle Kunden von ihrer Unparteilichkeit zu überzeugen. Es war auch die Zeit der Verdunkelung: Selbst der schmalste Lichtstreifen ließ die Wut eines

Luftschutzwartes über das jeweilige Haus hereinbrechen – was immer noch besser war als eine Bombe.

Kinder wurden aus den Städten auf das vergleichsweise sichere Land verschickt. Manche von ihnen freuten sich über die Veränderung, andere haßten sie. Einige marschierten gar immer wieder nach Hause zurück. Es kam auf das Kind an und darauf, wie es aufgenommen wurde.

Alte Männer und Knaben zogen Uniformen an und bewachten Kreuzungen, Eisenbahntunnel und die Küste. Jeder wurde angewiesen, seine Zunge zu hüten: „Gedankenloses Reden kostet Menschenleben".

Irgendwie gelang es der Zivilisation zu überleben – und noch bevor die vierziger Jahre vorüber waren, gab es sogar manche, die mit leiser Nostalgie auf die Kriegsjahre zurückblickten.

Ce fut la guerre des civils, les Heinkel, Halifax et Forteresses volantes répandant l'horreur dans les rues des banlieues et les centres des villes. Personne n'était épargné. L'abri dans le jardin et les quais d'une station de métro rappelaient en permanence que tout le monde était impliqué dans la lutte.

Il y avait des carnets de rationnement et on faisait la queue pour avoir à manger. S'il restait, ô surprise, quelques oignons, la nouvelle se répandait comme une traînée de poudre, et les bouchers et épiciers avaient bien du mal à convaincre chacun de leur impartialité. Et puis le couvre-feu : le moindre rayon de lumière faisait surgir dans la maison un contrôleur de raid aérien furieux – mais mieux valait cela qu'une bombe.

Les enfants furent transférés des villes vers la campagne, relativement sûre. Certains ont apprécié ce changement, d'autres l'ont haï. Quelques-uns sont rentrés chez eux à pied comme des chiens. Cela dépendant de l'enfant et de la nature de l'accueil reçu.

Des hommes âgés et des garçonnets portaient l'uniforme et surveillaient carrefour, littoral, tunnel de chemin de fer. On enseignait à chacun à tenir sa langue : «Les bavardages coûtent des vies humaines».

D'une façon ou d'une autre, la civilisation survécut. Et avant que les années quarante ne touchent à leur fin, certains repensèrent même aux années de guerre avec une pointe de nostalgie.

Though they were seldom needed in earnest, even on the Home Front everyone had to get used to wearing their gas mask.

Obwohl sie nur selten wirklich benötigt wurden, mußte sich selbst an der Heimatfront ein jeder daran gewöhnen, seine Gasmaske zu tragen.

Il était rare que l'on utilise sérieusement son masque à gaz; et pourtant, sur le front de l'intérieur, chacun devait s'habituer à le porter.

Two steelworkers
enjoy a cigarette
during a break from
work, November
1942. In peacetime,
few women would
have found work in
such a place.

Zwei Stahlarbeite-
rinnen genießen
während einer
Arbeitspause eine
Zigarette, November
1942. In
Friedenszeiten
hätten nur wenige
Frauen in einer
solchen Fabrik
Arbeit gefunden.

Deux ouvrières
d'une usine
sidérurgique fumant
une cigarette durant
une pause, en
novembre 1942.
En temps de paix,
bien peu de femmes
auraient trouvé un
emploi dans une
telle usine.

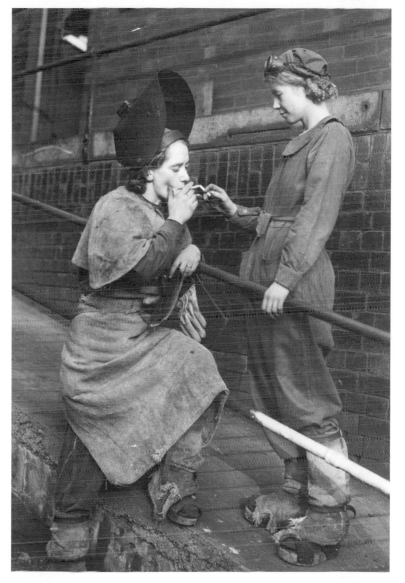

February 1941. Students work on a giant poster during Canterbury's 'Weapons Week'. 'Give us the tools' had become instantly famous as a slogan, although Churchill had coined the phrase only 12 days earlier.

Februar 1941. Studenten arbeiten an einem riesigen Plakat während der „Woche der Waffen" in Canterbury. „Gebt uns das Werkzeug" war im Handumdrehen zu einer bekannten Parole geworden, obwohl Churchill das Schlagwort erst 12 Tage zuvor geprägt hatte.

Février 1941. Etudiants réalisant une gigantesque affiche pour la «Semaine des armes», à Canterbury. «Donnez-nous les outils» devint instantanément une devise populaire, bien que Churchill ne l'ait lancée que 12 jours auparavant.

August 1940.
Hitler's last appeal
was dropped
from the skies.
Three weeks later
the Blitz began.

August 1940. Hitlers
letzter Appell an die
Vernunft der Briten
fiel vom Himmel
herab. Drei Wochen
später begann der
Luftangriff auf
britische Städte.

Août 1940. Le
dernier appel à la
raison lancé par
Hitler aux
Britanniques est
venu du ciel. Trois
semaines plus tard,
les bombes
tombaient sur les
villes de Grande-
Bretagne.

Dad's Army,
November 1942.
A member of the
25th Battalion
London Home
Guard demonstrates
the use of
camouflage.

Vaters Armee,
November 1942.
Ein Mitglied des
25. Bataillons der
Londoner Bürger-
wehr demonstriert
den Gebrauch von
Tarnung.

L'armée de père,
en novembre 1942.
Un membre du
25ᵉ Bataillon de
Territoriaux
londoniens fait une
démonstration de
camouflage.

After being the bogyman of Europe for decades, the Soviet Union suddenly became an heroic ally in 1941. A Red Cross representative collects money for the Russian war effort in the Strand, London on an 'Aid to Russia' flag day.

Nachdem sie jahrzehntelang das Schreckgespenst Europas gewesen war, wurde die Sowjetunion 1941 zu einer heldenhaften Verbündeten. Eine Mitarbeiterin des Roten Kreuzes sammelt in der Londoner Straße The Strand Geld zur Unterstützung der russischen Kriegsanstrengungen an einem besonderen „Hilfe für Rußland"-Sammeltag.

Après avoir été, durant des decennies, l'épouvantail de l'Europe, l'Union soviétique se mua soudain, en 1941, en un allié héroïque. Une bénévole de la Croix-Rouge collecte de l'argent dans le Strand, une rue de Londres, pour soutenir l'effort de guerre de la Russie lors d'une journée « Aidez la Russie ».

A huge campaign was mounted to save waste and recycle materials.
It was partly a morale-boosting exercise, to persuade civilians that
they could take an active part in the war. In this case, the message
was directed at the citizens of Cheltenham.

Die Regierung organisierte eine großangelegte Kampagne zur
Vermeidung von Abfällen und Wiederverwertung von Rohstoffen.
Auf diese Weise sollte der Zivilbevölkerung moralischer Auftrieb
gegeben und das Gefühl vermittelt werden, ebenfalls einen aktiven
Beitrag zum Kriegsgeschehen leisten zu können. Auf dieser Aufnahme
waren die Bürger von Cheltenham angesprochen.

On organisa des campagnes à grande échelle pour éviter les déchets
et récupérer les matières premières. Le but de la manœuvre était
notamment d'aider moralement la population civile en lui faisant
sentir qu'elle aussi pouvait contribuer activement à l'effort de guerre.
Dans le cas présent, le message s'adresse aux citoyens de Cheltenham.

Southgate, London, 1942. To prevent pedestrians colliding in the blackout, these slogans were stencilled on pavements all over the city.

Southgate, London, 1942. Um zu verhindern, daß Fußgänger während der Verdunkelung zusammenstießen, wurden in der ganzen Stadt Hinweise auf den Bürgersteigen angebracht.

Southgate, Londres, en 1942. Pour empêcher les collisions entre piétons pendant le couvre-feu, ce genre d'instructions étaient peintes sur les trottoirs de toute la ville: «Marcher sur la gauche du trottoir».

Rogue gift.
A volunteer holds a German helmet, mistakenly included in a collection of aluminium at the Chelsea Town Hall, July 1940.

Den Schalk im Nacken. Eine freiwillige Helferin im Juli 1940 mit einem deutschen Soldatenhelm, der fälschlicherweise bei einer Aluminium-Sammlung im Rathaus von Chelsea abgegeben wurde.

Sens de l'humour. Une auxiliaire bénévole avec un casque de soldat allemand remis par erreur lors d'une collecte d'aluminium à l'hôtel de ville de Chelsea, en juillet 1940.

Wrought-iron railings are removed from Battersea Park, London, 1940. The Government claimed they were melted down to provide metal for weapons. Later, the poor pointed out that similar gates and railings from the houses of the rich had been left alone.

Entfernung schmiedeeiserner Zäune im Battersea Park in London, 1940. Laut Regierung wurden sie eingeschmolzen, um Metall für die Waffenherstellung zu gewinnen. Später wiesen die Armen Londons darauf hin, daß ähnliche Tore und Zäune an den Häusern wohlhabender Bürger nicht angetastet worden waren.

Démontage de grilles en fer forgé au Battersea Park de Londres, en 1940.
Le gouvernement prétendait les fondre pour fabriquer des armes avec le métal. Plus tard, les pauvres de Londres rappelèrent que les portails et grilles de ce genre qui ornaient les maisons de riches citoyens étaient toujours debout.

Preparing for the Blitz, July 1940. Workers demonstrate the use of bomb 'snuffers' to extinguish incendiary bombs.

Juli 1940: Vorbereitung auf den deutschen Luftangriff Blitz. Arbeiter führen die Verwendung von „Bombenlöschern" vor, mit denen Brandbomben gelöscht werden sollten.

Juillet 1940: mesures préventives contre les attaques aériennes allemandes du Blitz. Ouvriers faisant une démonstration d'«extincteurs» de bombes censés éteindre les bombes incendiaires allemandes.

The wife of the inventor of the 'bomb grab' shows how your front parlour can be saved in seconds.

Die Ehefrau des Erfinders des „Bombengreifers" demonstriert, wie man sein Wohnzimmer innerhalb von Sekunden retten kann.

L'épouse de l'inventeur du « piège à bombes » indique comment sauver son salon en quelques secondes.

Mrs Whitham, mother of 16 children, tots up the 'points' in her family's ration books. The end of the war did not bring an end to rationing.

Mrs. Whitham, Mutter von 16 Kindern, rechnet die „Punkte" in den Bezugsscheinbüchern ihrer Familie zusammen. Das Ende des Krieges bedeutete nicht auch das Ende der Rationierung.

Mme Whitham, mère de 16 enfants, inscrit les « points » dans les carnets de rationnement de sa famille. La fin de la guerre n'a pas obligatoirement vu la fin du rationnement.

A shopkeeper tries to reassure customers. This picture was taken in February 1940. Within a short while many more items 'went on ration'.

Ein Ladenbesitzer versucht, seine Kunden zu beruhigen. Dieses Bild wurde im Februar 1940 aufgenommen. Kurze Zeit später wurden noch viele weitere Artikel rationiert.

Un épicier cherche à rassurer ses clients. Cette photo a été prise en février 1940. Peu de temps après, de nombreux autres articles furent rationnés.

'If you want to get ahead…' British troops fought in a vast variety of climates for king and country. Here a consignment of pith helmets, probably for India, receives a quality inspection before they are dispatched, August 1942.

„Du willst die Nase vorn haben? Gut, …" Britische Truppen kämpften unter den unterschiedlichsten klimatischen Bedingungen für König und Vaterland. Im August 1942 wird eine Ladung Tropenhelme, die wahrscheinlich für Indien bestimmt ist, vor dem Versand einer Qualitätskontrolle unterzogen.

« Tu veux garder la tête froide… » Les troupes britanniques se battaient sous toutes les latitudes imaginables pour leur roi et leur patrie. Cargaison de casques coloniaux, probablement destinés aux Indes, faisant l'objet d'un contrôle de qualité avant leur expédition, en août 1942.

'...get a hat.'
Women workers in a
factory add the final
touches to khaki
tam-o'-shanters for a
Scottish regiment,
September 1940.

„... dann kauf
dir einen Hut."
Arbeiterinnen in
einer Fabrik geben
im September 1940
khakifarbenen
schottischen
Baskenmützen für
ein schottisches
Regiment den letzten
Schliff.

«... alors achète-toi
un chapeau.»
Ouvrières d'usine
mettant la dernière
touche aux bérets
kaki destinés à un
régiment écossais, en
septembre 1940.

The Government struggled to reassure people at home that they could be
protected from air raids. Herbert Morrison, Minister of Home Security,
introduced the new indoor table shelter to the House of Commons in 1941.

Die Regierung gab sich große Mühe, der Bevölkerung zu versichern, daß
man sie vor Luftangriffen schützen konnte. Herbert Morrison, Minister für
Innere Sicherheit, stellte 1941 dem Unterhaus des Parlaments den neuen
Tisch-Bunker für das Wohnzimmer vor.

Le gouvernement ne ménageait aucun effort pour convaincre la population
civile que l'on pouvait se protéger contre les attaques aériennes. Herbert
Morrison, ministre de la Sécurité intérieure, présenta au Parlement cette
nouvelle table-abri de salon en 1941.

Family model.
Wembley Council
provided this
indoor shelter made
of timber and
corrugated iron in
January 1941.

Familienmodell.
Im Januar 1941
stellte der Stadtrat
von Wembley
Einwohnern diesen
Zimmerbunker
aus Bauholz und
Wellblech zur
Verfügung.

Modèle familial.
Le conseil municipal
de Wembley
présenta aux
habitants, en janvier
1941, cet abri de
chambre en bois de
charpente et tôle
ondulée.

Some shelters were built for only one. This structure was supplied as a refuge for the guardsman on duty outside Marlborough House, London in 1940. He may well have had to remove his busby to fit in it.

Manche Bunker wurden nur für eine Person gebaut. Diese Konstruktion wurde 1940 bereitgestellt, um dem diensthabenden Wachtposten vor Marlborough House in London Schutz zu gewähren. Er mußte wohl seine Bärenfellmütze abnehmen, um hineinzupassen.

Certains abris étaient conçus pour une seule personne. Ce modèle servait de refuge à la sentinelle de service devant Marlborough House, à Londres, en 1940. Il lui fallait sans doute ôter son couvre-chef pour y pénétrer.

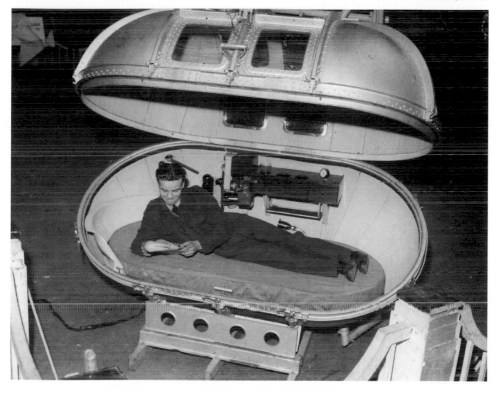

Special protection for a Very Important Person. This is the 'Churchill Egg', a pressurized cabin designed for the prime minister's private use when flying at a high altitude. If the great man smoked his cigars inside, it's a wonder he didn't asphyxiate himself.

Besonderer Schutz für eine besonders wichtige Person. Das „Churchill-Ei" ist eine auf Normaldruck gehaltene Kabine, die für den persönlichen Gebrauch des Premierministers auf Flügen in großer Höhe entwickelt wurde. Falls dieser bedeutende Mann hier seine Zigarren rauchte, ist es ein Wunder, daß er dabei nicht erstickte.

Protection spéciale pour VIP. L'«Œuf de Churchill», cabine pressurisée destinée à l'usage privé du Premier ministre lors de ses vols à haute altitude. Si le grand homme d'Etat fumait ses cigares à l'intérieur, il est étonnant qu'il n'ait pas péri asphyxié.

For houses without gardens, chains of street shelters were supplied. In 1941 there was no parking problem in a London street like this.

Für Häuser ohne Gärten wurden Straßenschutzbunker bereitgestellt. 1941 gab es in einer solchen Londoner Straße noch keine Parkprobleme.

Des abris de rue furent fabriqués à la chaîne pour les maisons sans jardin. En 1941, il n'y avait pas de problèmes de stationnement dans une rue de Londres comme celle-ci.

A typical scene in a
tube station during
the Blitz. Londoners
spend the night on a
stationary escalator.

Eine typische Szene
in einer U-Bahn-
Station zur Zeit
der deutschen
Luftangriffe.
Londoner Bürger
verbringen die Nacht
auf einer stillstehen-
den Rolltreppe.

Scène typique dans
une station de métro
durant le Blitz.
Londoniens passant
la nuit sur un
escalier mécanique
arrêté.

Councils were organized to run the London Underground shelters. Families had regular pitches. The platform was more comfortable than the stairs.

Es wurden Räte bestimmt, die für die Luftschutzkeller der Londoner U-Bahn verantwortlich waren. Familien hatten ihren bestimmten Stamm-platz. Die Bahnsteige waren bequemer als die Treppen.

Des comités furent organisés pour gérer les abris dans le métro londonien. Certaines familles avaient leur place habituelle. Le quai était plus confortable que les escaliers.

Muscovites shelter in the Maıakovskaia Underground station during the German bombardment in 1941. The stations were also used as hospitals.

Moskauer Bürger suchen Schutz in der U-Bahn-Station Majakowskaja während eines deutschen Bombenangriffs im Jahre 1941. Die Stationen dienten auch als Krankenhäuser.

Moscovites s'abritant à la station de métro de Maiakovskaia durant les bombardements allemands de 1941. Les stations servaient aussi d'hôpitaux.

Evacuated treasures.
A Goliath frog from
the Natural History
Museum finds a
wartime home in
Surrey caves, March
1943.

Evakuierte Schätze.
Ein Goliathfrosch
aus dem Museum
für Naturgeschichte
findet im März 1943
für die Dauer des
Krieges ein Zuhause
in einer Höhle in
Surrey.

Trésors évacués.
Une grenouille-
taureau du Museum
d'histoire naturelle
a trouvé refuge,
durant la guerre,
dans des caves du
Surrey, en mars
1943.

Sir Kenneth Clark, Director of the National Gallery, checks the well-being of some of the nation's masterpieces in their North Wales hideaway, 1942. The Gallery was emptied of its greatest paintings, but itself escaped damage.

Sir Kenneth Clark, Direktor der Nationalgalerie, prüft 1942 den Zustand einiger Meisterwerke aus Staatsbesitz in ihrem Versteck in Nordwales. Die berühmtesten Gemälde der Galerie waren zwar vorsorglich ausgelagert worden, doch das Gebäude überstand die Angriffe unbeschadet.

Sir Kenneth Clark, le directeur de la Galerie Nationale, vérifie le bon état de quelques chefs-d'œuvre nationaux, dans leur cachette du nord du pays de Galles, en 1942. Vidée de ses peintures les plus importantes, la Galerie Nationale ne subit elle-même aucun dommage.

The ruins of the old St Thomas's Hospital, London after an enemy raid. The hospital was heavily bombed and had to be completely rebuilt after the war. The Palace of Westminster also suffered, but not so disastrously.

Die Ruine des alten St. Thomas's Hospital in London nach einem feindlichen Angriff. Das Krankenhaus war stark zerbombt und mußte nach dem Krieg völlig neu wieder aufgebaut werden. Der Palast von Westminster hatte auch gelitten, allerdings nicht in diesem Ausmaß.

Les ruines du vieil hôpital Saint-Thomas, à Londres, après un raid ennemi. Gravement bombardé, l'hôpital dut être complètement reconstruit après la guerre. Le palais de Westminster a lui aussi souffert, mais pas de façon aussi dramatique.

Soldiers clear the rubble from the Bank Underground station. Like St Paul's Cathedral, the Mansion House (in the background) sustained only slight damage.

Soldaten beseitigen die Trümmer über der U-Bahn-Station Bank. Ebenso wie die Kathedrale St. Paul's war das Mansion House (im Hintergrund) nur leicht beschädigt.

Soldats dégageant les gravats devant la station de métro du Bank. Comme la cathédrale Saint-Paul, Mansion House (à l'arrière-plan) ne subit pas de dommages sérieux.

Balham High Street,
October 1940.
A witness of the
Blitz wrote, 'The
earth seemed to
split into a thousand
fragments.'

Balham High Street,
Oktober 1940.
Ein Zeuge des
Luftangriffs schrieb:
„Die Erde schien in
tausend Stücke zu
zerbrechen".

Balham High Street,
en octobre 1940.
Un témoin du Blitz
écrivit: « La terre
sembla éclater en
milliers de
fragments ».

Canterbury, June 1942. A newly homeless family sets out to find somewhere to live.

Canterbury, Juni 1942. Eine ausgebombte Familie beginnt, nach einer neuen Bleibe zu suchen.

Canterbury, juin 1942. Une famille qui vient de perdre son domicile recherche un endroit pour s'installer.

Wedding Day, 1940. It became a matter of
pride on all home fronts that everything
in life and business should carry on as usual.
The marriage rate actually increased.
Men and women saw getting married during
the war as an act of faith.

Hochzeitstag, 1940. An sämtlichen Heimat-
fronten wurde es zu einer Frage des Stolzes,
das Leben und die Geschäfte wie gewohnt
weiterzuführen. Die Zahl der Eheschlie-
ßungen nahm sogar zu. Männer wie Frauen
betrachteten eine Heirat zu Kriegszeiten
als einen Vertrauensbeweis.

Noce, en 1940. Faire que la vie continue
comme si de rien n'était était une question
d'honneur sur le front intérieur. Et le taux
des mariages augmenta réellement. Hommes
et femmes estimaient que se marier durant
la guerre était un acte de foi.

London, October 1940. While firemen damp down the smouldering ruins behind him,
a milkman picks his way through rubble to deliver the morning's supply. Churchill's words
to Hitler voiced the feelings of many Londoners: 'You do your worst – and we will do our best.'

London, Oktober 1940. Während Feuerwehrleute die Glut der schwelenden Ruinen hinter
ihm ersticken, sucht ein Milchmann seinen Weg durch die Trümmer, um die morgendliche
Lieferung auszutragen. „Sie tun das Schlimmste – und wir tun unser Bestes", sagte Churchill
zu Hitler und spiegelte damit die Meinung vieler Londoner wider.

Londres, octobre 1940. Pendant que des pompiers éteignent les ruines fumantes derrière lui,
un laitier escalade les gravats pour faire sa tournée matinale. Les mots de Churchill à Hitler,
« Vous faites le pire – et nous faisons de notre mieux », exprimaient les sentiments de nombreux
Londoniens.

Old Kent Road,
London, September
1940. Business as
usual for a postman
collecting mail from
a battered pillar box.

Old Kent Road,
London, September
1940. Ein Post-
beamter geht wie
immer seiner Arbeit
nach und leert einen
beschädigten Brief-
kasten.

Old Kent Road,
septembre 1940.
Comme à
l'accoutumée, un
postier fait la levée
dans une boîte
aux lettres
endommagée.

Dressed more for the camera than her surroundings, artist Ethel Gabain paints a scene of air raid damage for the Ministry of Information, November 1940. The Government believed that paintings often served better than photographs as propaganda.

Eher für die Kamera als zu ihrer Umgebung passend angezogen malt die Künstlerin Ethel Gabain für das Informationsministerium den Schauplatz eines Luftangriffs im November 1940. Die Regierung war der Meinung, daß Gemälde oft besser als Fotos den Zwecken der Propaganda dienten.

Bien habillée à l'attention du photographe et plantée dans un décor de ruines, l'artiste Ethel Gabain peint une scène de décombres après un raid aérien pour le ministère de l'Information, en novembre 1940. Le gouvernement croyait que les peintures servaient mieux la propagande que les photographies.

'Business as usual' at its most absurd. Readers browse among the charred remains of the Earl of Ilchester's library at Holland House in 1941. The house was so badly damaged that it was left derelict until 1952.

„Normaler Alltag" in seiner absurdesten Form. Leser schmökern 1941 in den verkohlten Resten der Bibliothek des Grafen von Ilchester im Holland House. Das Haus wurde so schwer beschädigt, daß es erst nach 1952 wiederaufgebaut wurde.

« La vie continue » dans son expression la plus absurde. Lecteurs inspectant les rayons dévastés de la bibliothèque du Comte d'Ilchester, à Holland House, en 1941. L'édifice a été si gravement endommagé qu'il ne fut reconstruit qu'en 1952.

The men who captured the news – good or bad. Fred
Ramage at work during the foggy days of 1946. Several
of the photographs in chapter 5 were taken by him.

Die Männer, die die Nachrichten einfingen – ob gute
oder schlechte. Fred Ramage bei der Arbeit an den
nebligen Tagen des Jahres 1946. Einige Aufnahmen in
Kapitel 5 stammen von ihm.

L'homme qui faisait l'information – bonne ou
mauvaise. Fred Ramage au travail par un matin
brumeux de 1946. Il a réalisé certaines des
photographies du chapitre 5.

Reporters dash to the phones to file their copy after hearing sentences passed on Nazi war criminals at the Palace of Justice, Nuremberg, in 1946. The trials began in November 1945 and lasted until 1947.

Reporter spurten nach der Urteilsverkündung über national-sozialistische Kriegsverbrecher im Nürnberger Justizpalast 1946 zu den Telefonen, um ihre Berichte durchzugeben. Die Nürnberger Prozesse begannen im November 1945 und dauerten bis 1947 an.

Reporters se précipitant vers les téléphones pour transmettre leur article après avoir entendu les jugements rendus contre les criminels de guerre nazis au Palais de justice de Nuremberg en 1946. Les procès ont commencé en 1945 et se sont terminés en 1947.

The last desperate gamble. In 1944 the Nazis began their V1 and V2 flying bomb raids on London and the Home Counties. Here a man is rescued from the wreckage of his London home.

Der letzte, verzweifelte Versuch zu gewinnen. 1944 beginnen die Nazis den V1- und V2-Waffen-Beschuß auf London und die angrenzenden Grafschaften. Auf dieser Aufnahme wird gerade ein Mann aus den Trümmern seines Londoner Hauses geborgen.

Dernier geste désespéré. En 1944, les nazis ont commencé à lancer leurs bombes volantes V1 et V2 sur Londres et les comtés environnants. Ici, un homme est évacué des ruines de son domicile londonien.

This V2 rocket
attack killed
300 civilians in
Farringdon Market,
London, March
1945.

Dieser V-2-Angriff
im März 1945
tötete 300 Zivilisten
im Londoner
Farringdon Market.

Ce raid de fusées
V2 a tué 300 civils
au marché de
Farringdon, à
Londres, en mars
1945.

The cost of liberation, December 1944. A Dutch boy stands in front of the wreckage of his home.

Der Preis der Befreiung, Dezember 1944. Ein holländischer Junge steht vor der Ruine seines Elternhauses.

Le prix de la libération, décembre 1944. Un jeune Hollandais devant ce qui reste de son foyer.

The cost of defeat,
July 1945.
Berliners, with the
few possessions
they have left,
in the ruins of the
Nollendorfplatz.

Der Preis der Nie-
derlage, Juli 1945.
Berliner Bürger mit
den wenigen ge-
retteten Habselig-
keiten zwischen den
Überresten des
Nollendorfplatzes.

Le prix de la défaite,
juillet 1945.
Berlinois avec les
quelques biens qu'ils
ont pu sauver, dans
les ruines de la place
de Nollendorf.

And all for £3 a week. A fireman tackles a blaze 80 feet (25 metres) above a London street, February 1941.

Und all das für 3 Pfund die Woche. Ein Feuerwehrmann bekämpft im Februar 1941 ein Feuer in 25 Meter Höhe über einer Londoner Straße.

Et tout ça pour trois livres par semaine. Un pompier éteint un incendie à 25 mètres de hauteur, dans une rue de Londres, en février 1941.

Local civilian women firefighters struggling to control the fires that raged in Pearl Harbor after the Japanese attack, 7 December 1941. Twenty-two warships were sunk or damaged, 200 planes destroyed, 2,400 people killed.

Ortsansässige zivile Feuerwehrfrauen versuchen, die Feuersbrünste unter Kontrolle zu bekommen, die in Pearl Harbor nach dem Angriff der Japaner am 7. Dezember 1941 wüteten. 22 Kriegsschiffe wurden versenkt oder beschädigt, 200 Flugzeuge zerstört und 2.400 Menschen getötet.

Femmes pompiers bénévoles cherchant à éteindre les incendies qui font rage à Pearl Harbor après l'attaque japonaise du 7 décembre 1941. 2 400 personnes furent tuées, 22 bâtiments de guerre coulés ou endommagés, 200 avions détruits.

Undesirable aliens. American police search a bewildered group of
Japanese residents. The Japanese were seen as potential saboteurs by
the US authorities, even in the days before the attack on Pearl Harbor.

Unerwünschte Ausländer. Amerikanische Polizisten durchsuchen
verwunderte japanische Einwohner. Die US-Behörden sahen in allen
Japanern potentielle Saboteure, sogar in der Zeit vor dem Angriff auf
Pearl Harbor.

Etrangers indésirables. La police américaine contrôle un groupe de
résidents japonais désorientés. Les autorités américaines considéraient
les Japonais comme des saboteurs potentiels même durant les jours
qui ont précédé l'attaque contre Pearl Harbor.

In Britain, people of Italian and German origin were rounded
up and interned. A group of women aliens are escorted by police to
a London station, on the way to camps on the Isle of Man.

In Großbritannien wurden Menschen italienischer und deutscher
Herkunft ausfindig gemacht und interniert. Die Polizei eskortiert
eine Gruppe von Ausländerinnen zu einem Londoner Bahnhof, von
wo sie in verschiedene Lager auf der Isle of Man gebracht werden.

En Grande-Bretagne, les personnes d'origine italienne ou allemande
furent rassemblées et internées. Des agents de police escortent
un groupe de femmes étrangères jusqu'à une gare de Londres, à
destination d'un des camps de l'île de Man.

In 1941 the British Government took the unprecedented step of
conscripting women for war service. The main opponents of this step
were men, women in general accepted it. Here women born in 1919
register at a labour exchange.

1941 zog die britische Regierung erstmals Frauen zum Kriegsdienst ein.
Die Hauptgegner dieser Maßnahme waren Männer; Frauen hingegen
akzeptierten sie im allgemeinen. Hier lassen sich Frauen des Jahrgangs
1919 in einem Arbeitsamt erfassen.

En 1941, le gouvernement britannique prit une mesure sans précédent:
la conscription des femmes pour la guerre. Les opposants les plus virulents
à cette mesure étaient les hommes; les femmes, en général, l'acceptèrent.
Ici, des femmes nées en 1919 s'inscrivent dans un bureau du travail.

Members of the ATS service a six-wheel truck at an army depot.
By 1944 over half a million British women were serving in the armed
forces, and millions more had been drafted into the Land Army and
factories.

Mitglieder des Auxiliary Territorial Service (ATS) bei der Wartung eines
Lastkraftwagens in einem Militärdepot. 1944 dienten über eine halbe
Million britische Frauen in den Streitkräften, und weitere Millionen
waren zur Landwehr und zum Dienst in Fabriken einberufen worden.

Des auxiliaires femmes travaillant sur un camion à six roues dans un
dépôt de l'armée. En 1944, plus de 500 000 citoyennes britanniques
servaient dans les forces armées et des millions d'autres avaient été
recrutées pour l'armée et les usines.

Seaside danger.
An elderly woman
examines a mine
washed up on the
east coast of
England, April 1940.

Gefahr am Strand.
Eine ältere Dame
untersucht im April
1940 eine Mine, die
an der Ostküste
Englands ange-
schwemmt wurde.

Le littoral, source de
danger. Une femme
âgée examine une
mine échouée sur la
côte est de
l'Angleterre en avril
1940.

Country safety.
A mother and baby
prepare to leave
London, November
1940. The mother is
carrying a special gas
mask for babies.

Sicherheit auf dem
Land. Im November
1940 bereitet sich
eine Mutter darauf
vor, London mit
ihrem Kind zu
verlassen. In der
Hand trägt sie eine
spezielle Gasmaske
für Babys.

La campagne, havre
de sécurité. Une
mère et son bébé se
préparent à quitter
Londres en
novembre 1940.
La mère porte un
masque à gaz spécial
pour bebés.

Mixing with the locals. A GI gains the undivided attention of a
waitress at Rainbow Corner, Piccadilly Circus, in January 1944. The
café was established as a venue for American service personnel.

Man mischt sich unter die Einheimischen. Ein GI hat im Januar
1944 die ungeteilte Aufmerksamkeit einer Kellnerin im Rainbow
Corner am Piccadilly Circus. Dieses Café wurde als Treffpunkt für
amerikanische Militärangehörige eingerichtet.

Contact avec la population locale. Un GI bénéficie de l'attention
sans partage d'une serveuse au Rainbow Corner, à Piccadilly Circus,
en janvier 1944. Ce café était un lieu de rendez-vous pour les
militaires américains.

Safe return. A member of the British Expeditionary Force receives an ecstatic welcome from his girlfriend on his return from Dunkirk. 'Operation Dynamo' was, in Churchill's words, 'a miracle of deliverance'. Over 330,000 men were rescued.

Wieder daheim und unverletzt. Ein Mitglied des britischen Expeditionskorps wird bei seiner Rückkehr aus Dünkirchen von seiner Freundin überglücklich begrüßt. Die „Operation Dynamo" war, in Churchills Worten, „ein Befreiungswunder". Über 330.000 Mann wurden gerettet.

De retour sain et sauf. Un membre du corps expéditionnaire britannique reçoit un baiser de bienvenue passionné à son retour de Dunkerque. L'« opération Dynamo » a été, suivant les propres mots de Churchill, « le miracle de la délivrance ». Plus de 330 000 hommes furent sauvés.

As the build-up of men and equipment for D-day reaches its height, US troops join in a children's game 'somewhere in the south of England'. Most people knew the invasion of Europe was imminent, but few guessed where it would take place.

Während die Vorbereitungen für den Tag X ihren Höhepunkt erreichen, schließen sich amerikanische Soldaten „irgendwo im Süden Englands" spontan einem Kinderspiel an. Die meisten Menschen wußten, daß die Invasion Europas unmittelbar bevorstand, doch die wenigsten vermuteten, wo sie stattfinden würde.

Alors que la concentration des hommes et du matériel en vue du Jour J va bientôt culminer, les soldats américains jouent avec des enfants « quelque part dans le sud de l'Angleterre ». La plupart des gens savaient que l'invasion de l'Europe était imminente, mais ils furent rares à deviner où elle aurait lieu.

The Pheasantry Club, London, 1940. Pre-war night clubs survived and even prospered during the war. Whisky and champagne were occasionally in short supply, but the bands played on and there were always plenty of dance partners.

Der Pheasantry Club, London, 1940. Nachtclubs aus der Zeit vor dem Krieg überlebten und florierten sogar während des Krieges. Gelegentlich wurden Whisky und Champagner knapp, doch die Musikkapellen spielten weiter, und Tanzpartner gab es stets im Überfluß.

Pheasantry Club, Londres, 1940. Les boîtes de nuit survécurent et prospérèrent même durant la guerre. On était parfois à court de whisky et de champagne, mais les orchestres jouaient de la musique et les cavaliers étaient innombrables.

Night clubs were prohibitively expensive for the masses. They flocked instead to the local dance halls, where the bands were as good, the floor as packed, and the opportunities for romance every bit as enticing.

Für die Massen war der Besuch von Nachtclubs unerschwinglich teuer. Statt dessen strömten sie in die örtlichen Tanzsäle, wo die Kapellen genauso gut spielten, das Parkett nicht minder überfüllt war und die Chancen für einen Flirt ebenso verlockend schienen.

Les boîtes de nuit étaient beaucoup trop chères pour la plupart des gens. Ils préféraient se réunir dans de vastes salles de bal, où les orchestres étaient aussi bons, le plancher aussi ciré et les possibilités de flirt tout aussi excitantes.

# 3. Tools and training
## Ausrüstung und Ausbildung
## Outils et formation

Sailors of the British Navy prepare to drop their cargo of
mines, 1940. In the early part of the war German U-boats,
operating from French ports, had the upper hand in the
war at sea. At the height of the Battle of the Atlantic up to
700,000 tons of shipping were sunk in a single month.

Im Jahre 1940 bereiten sich Matrosen der britischen
Marine darauf vor, ihre Minenfracht abzuwerfen.
Zu Kriegsbeginn behielten deutsche U-Boote, die von
französischen Häfen aus operierten, im Seekrieg die
Oberhand. Als die Schlacht im Atlantik ihren Gipfelpunkt
erreichte, wurden innerhalb eines Monats Schiffe in einem
Gesamtgewicht von etwa 700.000 Tonnen versenkt.

Des marins de la British Navy s'apprêtent à immerger
leur cargaison de mines, en 1940. Au début de la guerre,
les sous-marins allemands opérant depuis les ports
français avaient la mainmise sur la guerre en haute mer.
Au summum de la bataille de l'Atlantique, ils coulèrent
jusqu'à 700 000 tonnes de bâtiments en un seul mois.

# 3. Tools and training
## Ausrüstung und Ausbildung
## Outils et formation

With the exception of the Pacific theatre, World War II was fought in the northern hemisphere in what is today called the 'developed world'. Here whole economies were turned over to war production. The entire populations and all the resources of Italy, France, Germany, Britain, the Soviet Union and the United States were devoted to supplying the guns or firing them.

Politicians and generals alike screamed for more planes, ships, tanks. At times of crisis, quantity control was more important than quality control. With millions of men engaged in combat, women now played a key role in keeping the weapons coming.

There was work to be done that people had never dreamed of doing: fire-fighting, plane-spotting, billeting children and displaced persons, running tea and coffee stalls for returning troops. Women who had been in domestic service suddenly found themselves aiming anti-aircraft guns, men who had worked in 'gentlemen's outfitting' learnt how to kill.

When the war was all over, and the swords were turned back into ploughshares, millions had to be retrained, factories had to be re-tooled. As for the women who had worked in farms and factories, most went back to being housewives.

Mit Ausnahme des Kriegsschauplatzes im Pazifik fanden die Kämpfe des Zweiten Weltkrieges in der nördlichen Hemisphäre statt, in der sogenannten „entwickelten Welt". Ganze Wirtschaftssysteme wurden hier auf die Produktion von Kriegsmaterial umgestellt. Die gesamte Bevölkerung und alle Ressourcen Italiens, Frankreichs, Deutschlands, Großbritanniens, der Sowjetunion und der Vereinigten Staaten dienten der Beschaffung von Waffen oder deren Einsatz.

Politiker wie Generäle forderten mehr Flugzeuge, mehr Schiffe und mehr Panzer, denn in Krisenzeiten war Quantität wichtiger als Qualität. Da Millionen von Männern für das Vaterland kämpften, spielten nun die Frauen eine entscheidende Rolle bei der kontinuierlichen Versorgung mit Waffen.

Jeder mußte mit anpacken. Nun galt es, Feuersbrünste zu bekämpfen, Flugzeuge zu sichten und zu erkennen, Quartiere für Kinder und Flüchtlinge zu suchen oder Tee- und Kaffeestände für heimkehrende Soldaten zu betreiben. Hausmädchen zielten plötzlich mit Flakgeschützen; Herrenausstatter lernten zu töten.

Als der Krieg endgültig vorbei war, und die Schwerter wieder in Pflugscharen verwandelt wurden, mußten Millionen von Menschen umgeschult und Fabriken mit neuen Maschinen ausgerüstet werden. Die Frauen, die auf Bauernhöfen und in Fabriken gearbeitet hatten, kehrten größtenteils wieder ins Hausfrauendasein zurück.

A l'exception du théâtre du Pacifique, la Seconde Guerre mondiale s'est déroulée dans l'hémisphère Nord, ce que nous appelons aujourd'hui le « monde développé ». Là, des économies entières se sont consacrées à la production militaire. Les populations entières et toutes les ressources de l'Italie, de la France, de l'Allemagne, de la Grande-Bretagne, de l'Union soviétique et des Etats-Unis furent mises à profit pour fabriquer canons ou munitions.

Hommes politiques et généraux réclamaient sans cesse de nouveaux avions, bateaux et blindés. En période de crise, le contrôle de la quantité était plus important que celui de la qualité. Des millions d'hommes étant engagés sur le front, ce furent désormais les femmes qui jouèrent un rôle clef pour assurer la production des armes.

Il fallait accomplir des travaux que nul n'aurait imaginé faire un jour : combattre les incendies, repérer les avions, loger des enfants et personnes déplacées, tenir des stands de thé et de café pour les troupes de retour du front. D'anciennes employées de maison se retrouvèrent soudain dirigeant des canons de DCA, et des hommes qui avaient exercé des « métiers de gentlemen » apprirent à tuer.

La guerre terminée et les épées transformées en socs de charrue, il fallut redonner une formation à des millions de gens, rééquiper des milliers d'usines. Quant aux femmes qui avaient travaillé dans des fermes et des usines, elles retournèrent, pour la plupart, à leur état de ménagères.

Workers in a Lancashire factory stack barbed wire made from scrap metal. It was sent to France to protect the Allies from German invasion in 1940.

Arbeiter in einer Fabrik in Lancashire stapeln Stacheldraht aus Altmetall, der 1940 nach Frankreich gesandt wurde, um die Alliierten vor der deutschen Invasion zu schützen.

Ouvriers d'une usine du Lancashire entassant des rouleaux de fil de fer barbelé fabriqué avec du métal recyclé. Ils étaient destinés à la France pour protéger les alliés contre l'invasion allemande en 1940.

Women munition-
workers in 1942.
In World War I
their mothers and
grandmothers would
probably have played
a less active role in
the war effort.

Arbeiterinnen einer
Waffen- und Muni-
tionsfabrik im Jahre
1942. Ihre Mütter
und Großmütter
hatten bei den
Kriegsanstrengungen
des Ersten Weltkrie-
ges wahrscheinlich
eine weniger aktive
Rolle gespielt.

Ouvrières dans une
usine de munitions,
en 1942. Durant la
Première Guerre
mondiale, leurs
mères et grands-
mères avaient sans
doute joué un rôle
moins actif dans les
efforts de guerre.

By 1940 the demand for women workers in Ministry of Supply factories was enormous. Churchill called for a million volunteers.

Bis 1940 war der Bedarf an Arbeiterinnen in den Fabriken des Versorgungsministeriums enorm angestiegen. Churchill rief eine Million Freiwillige zur Unterstützung auf.

En 1940, la demande d'ouvrières dans les usines du ministère de l'Approvisionnement fut gigantesque. Churchill réclama un million de volontaires.

Women were quick to learn the skills needed to produce weapons and ammunition. Here a woman is fitting the Caterpillar track on a tank. Her foreman may well have wondered what the world was coming to if he examined her footwear.

Frauen erlernten schnell die handwerklichen Fertigkeiten, um Waffen und Munition herstellen zu können. Hier bringt eine Frau eine Raupenkette an einem Panzer an. Ihr Vorarbeiter hätte sich wohl über die Zeiten gewundert, wenn er ihr Schuhwerk inspiziert hätte.

Les femmes apprenaient très vite à fabriquer armes et munitions. Ici, l'une d'entre elles monte une chenille sur un blindé. Son chef d'atelier s'est sans doute demandé où allait le monde en voyant les chaussures portées au travail par son ouvrière.

By 1941 Britain's railways were in crisis. They were having to carry goods that had previously travelled by sea, more passengers than ever before (as a result of petrol rationing), and weapons of war from the factories in the north to the ports in the south.

1941 befand sich die britische Eisenbahn bereits in einem Engpaß. Sie mußte nicht nur Güter befördern, die früher verschifft worden waren, sondern auch mehr Passagiere als je zuvor (ein Ergebnis der Benzinrationierung) sowie Kriegswaffen von den Fabriken im Norden zu den Häfen im Süden.

En 1941, les chemins de fer britanniques étaient en pleine crise. Ils devaient transporter des marchandises jusqu'ici acheminées par voie maritime et plus de voyageurs que jamais auparavant (par suite du rationnement des carburants) ainsi que des armes de guerre des usines du Nord jusqu'aux ports du Sud.

Lancaster bombers are assembled at a factory near Manchester, September 1943. They were the first of the long-range British bombers, and were used to attack targets deep in enemy territory.

Bombenflugzeuge des Typs Lancaster werden im September 1943 in einer Fabrik in der Nähe von Manchester montiert. Dies waren die ersten britischen Langstreckenbomber, mit denen tief im feindlichen Territorium gelegene Ziele angegriffen wurden.

Bombardiers Lancaster en cours de montage dans une usine proche de Manchester, en septembre 1943. Ce furent les premiers bombardiers britanniques à long rayon d'action utilisés pour attaquer des cibles au cœur du territoire ennemi.

Primitive methods, modern weapons. War workers add explosives to bomb casings. The British munitions industry lived a hand-to-mouth existence in 1940.

Primitive Methoden, moderne Waffen. Kriegsarbeiterinnen füllen Bomben-mäntel mit Spreng-stoff. Die britische Munitionsindustrie lebte 1940 von der Hand in den Mund.

Méthodes primitives, arts modernes. Des ouvrières versent des explosifs dans le cylindre d'une bombe. En 1940, l'industrie des munitions britannique était extrêmement précaire.

Keep fit exercises, 1941 style. A woman casually rolls a bomb across the factory floor in Bert Hardy's photograph.

Fitneßgymnastik im Stil von 1941. Bert Hardys Aufnahme zeigt eine Frau, die lässig eine Bombe über den Fabrikboden rollt.

Faire de l'exercice pour garder la forme à la mode de 1941. Une femme fait rouler élégamment une bombe sur le sol d'une usine, sur une photographie de Bert Hardy.

German children play among rows of shells
awaiting collection in a Munich street, May 1943.
It wasn't until after 1943 that Allied bombing
made any significant reduction in German
manufacture and production of war materials.

Im Mai 1943 spielen deutsche Kinder zwischen
Granaten, die in einer Straße in München darauf
warten, abgeholt zu werden. Erst nach 1943
bewirkten Bombenangriffe der Alliierten eine
nennenswerte Verringerung der Herstellung von
Kriegsmaterialien in Deutschland.

Des enfants allemands jouent entre des rangées
d'obus devant être collectés dans une rue de
Munich, en mai 1943. Il n'a pas fallu attendre
1943 pour que les bombardements alliés
entraînent une réduction significative de la
production de matériel militaire en Allemagne.

Hand grenades on an assembly line in Moscow, 1942. The
Soviet Union ran a quota system for each factory, challenging
workers to exceed the production expected of them.

Handgranaten auf einem Montagetisch in Moskau, 1942.
Die Sowjetunion unterhielt in jeder Fabrik ein Quoten-
system, um die Arbeiter zu motivieren, die von ihnen
erwartete Produktionsmenge zu übertreffen.

Grenades en cours de montage à Moscou, en 1942. L'Union
soviétique instaura un système de quotas pour chaque usine,
lançant aux ouvriers un défi pour les inciter à dépasser la
production escomptée.

Russian women grease artillery shells by hand before dispatch to the front. In 1942 the Soviet Union was fighting for its very existence, with Leningrad and Stalingrad besieged, and Moscow itself under threat.

Russische Frauen fetten Artilleriegranaten von Hand ein, bevor sie an die Front versandt werden. 1942 kämpfte die Sowjetunion ums nackte Überleben, denn Leningrad und Stalingrad wurden belagert, und selbst Moskau war in Gefahr.

Femmes russes graissant des obus d'artillerie à la main avant de les expédier au front. En 1942, l'Union soviétique se battait pour sa propre existence, Leningrad et Stalingrad étant assiégées et Moscou elle-même menacée.

In 1940, rifles that the British troops of 1914 would have recognized are stacked from a wheelbarrow at the Royal Ordnance Factory. Many months were to pass before the British supply system reached the required efficiency.

1940 werden Gewehre, die britische Soldaten von 1914 wiedererkannt hätten, in der Königlichen Munitionsfabrik von einem Schubkarren abgeladen und geordnet. Es sollten viele Monate vergehen, bis das britische Versorgungssystem die erforderliche Effizienz erreichte.

En 1940, des fusils que les troupes britanniques de 1914 auraient immédiatement reconnus sont déchargés d'un diable à la Royal Ordnance Factory. Il fallut plusieurs mois pour que le système d'approvisionnement britannique devienne vraiment efficace.

A Canadian worker fits transparent hoods over the landing lights of Harvard monoplanes. Many Commonwealth pilots trained on the Harvard.

Ein kanadischer Arbeiter montiert transparente Kappen über die Landebeleuchtung von Eindeckern des Typs Harvard. Viele Piloten des Commonwealth wurden auf der Harvard ausgebildet.

Un ouvrier canadien monte des carénages transparents sur les phares d'atterrissage de monoplans Harvard. De nombreux pilotes du Commonwealth se sont entraînés sur des Harvard.

London firemen pack the galleries to watch the final of the Auxiliary
Fire Service trailer pump competition, March 1940. A tougher
test was to come for the AFS later that year when the Blitz began.

Londoner Feuerwehrleute drängen sich auf den Rängen, um das
Wettbewerbsfinale der Hilfstruppe der Feuerwehr im März 1940
mitzuerleben. Ein härterer Test für den AFS sollte im gleichen Jahr
mit dem Beginn des Blitz' folgen.

Des pompiers londoniens aux balcons pour assister à la finale des
concours de gymnastique des pompiers auxiliaires, en mars 1940.
Ils allaient devoir relever un défi autrement plus difficile, moins d'un
an plus tard, lorsque débuta le Blitz.

Fitness training before the Battle of Britain. Young RAF recruits keep their guard up, February 1940.

Fitneßtraining vor der großen Schlacht um England. Junge Rekruten der britischen Luftwaffe achten im Februar 1940 auf gute Deckung.

Culture physique avant la bataille d'Angleterre. De jeunes recrues de la RAF se mettent en garde, en février 1940.

What a way to win a war! Royal Air Force cadets learn the art of
formation flying on bicycles, June 1942. No matter how hard they
pedalled, the wings were never large enough to enable them to take off.

Was für eine Art, einen Krieg zu gewinnen! Kadetten der britischen
Luftwaffe erlernen im Juni 1942 auf Fahrrädern die Kunst des Forma-
tionsfliegens. Doch so sehr sie auch strampeln mochten – die Flügel
waren einfach nicht groß genug, um abheben zu können.

Drôle de façon de gagner la guerre ! Les cadets de la Royal Air Force
apprennent à voler en formation à l'aide de bicyclettes, en juin 1942.
Ils pouvaient pédaler de toutes leurs forces, leurs ailes n'étaient jamais
assez grandes pour les faire décoller.

A sporting chance. RAF gunners train by aiming their gun at a moving target. Unsportingly, German Fokkers and Messerschmitts tended to appear out of the clouds moving considerably faster.

Eine faire Chance. Artilleristen der britischen Luftwaffe üben, ihr Geschütz auf ein bewegliches Ziel auszurichten. Unfairerweise neigten deutsche Fokker- und Messerschmitt-Flugzeuge dazu, mit beträchtlich höherer Geschwindigkeit aus den Wolken aufzutauchen.

En joue, feu ! Des artilleurs de la RAF apprennent à viser sur une cible mobile. Dans un esprit peu sportif, les Fokker et autres Messerschmitt allemands avaient en effet l'habitude de surgir sournoisement des nuages à la vitesse de l'éclair.

Fit for battle. Much of the basic training of recruits was concerned with improving physical fitness. The emphasis on precision was often an attempt to keep morale high. Rivalry between different units was sometimes fiercer than hatred of the enemy.

Fit für die Schlacht. Die Grundausbildung der Rekruten bestand größtenteils aus körperlicher Ertüchtigung. Die präzise Ausführung der Übungen sollte die Truppen bei guter Moral halten. Die Rivalität unter den verschiedenen Einheiten war manchmal größer als die Abscheu vor dem Feind.

En forme pour la bataille. Une grande partie de la formation de base des recrues consistait à améliorer leur constitution physique. L'accent mis sur la précision avait souvent pour but de leur faire garder le moral. La rivalité entre les différentes unités était parfois plus acharnée et plus prononcée que la haine envers l'ennemi.

A gymnastic display by soldiers recovering at a military convalescence depot in south-east England, 1940.

Eine Gymnastik-vorführung von Soldaten in einem militärischen Genesungslager im Südosten Englands, 1940.

Démonstration de gymnastique par des soldats en convalescence dans un établissement militaire du sud-est de l'Angleterre, en 1940.

# 4. Heading for peace
# Auf dem Weg zum Frieden
# Avancée pour la paix

Paul Tibbets waves from the cockpit of *Enola Gay*, the B-29 Superfortress that dropped the first atomic bomb on Japan. The plane was named after Tibbets' mother. The bomb wiped out four square miles (10 square kilometres) of Hiroshima.

Paul Tibbets winkt aus dem Cockpit der *Enola Gay*, der B-29-Superfortress, die die erste Atombombe über Japan abwarf. Das Flugzeug war nach Tibbets' Mutter benannt. Die Bombe machte 10 Quadratkilometer der Stadt Hiroshima dem Erdboden gleich.

Paul Tibbets saluant, depuis le cockpit d'*Enola Gay*, la Super Forteresse B-29 qui largua la première bombe atomique sur le Japon. L'avion fut baptisé du nom de la mère de Tibbets. La bombe réduisit à néant 10 kilomètres carrés d'Hiroshima.

# 4. Heading for peace
# Auf dem Weg zum Frieden
# Avancée pour la paix

The tide of war turned. It became not a question of who would win, but how long the losers could keep going. Village by village across Normandy, more rapidly across great swathes of Eastern Europe, the fighting pushed closer to Berlin. Mussolini's strutting reign in Italy came to a shocking end. City after city, camp after camp was liberated from Fascist control.

Partisans hastened the process. Gradually they ceased to be silent, secret organizations that struck by night. They emerged into the open, taking over increasingly large sections of their homeland as the occupying troops retreated.

In the Far East the sun began to sink over the Japanese empire. The fighting here was some of the bitterest in the whole war – every island became a battleground, losses on both sides were appalling. And then came the final monstrous explosions that dealt a death-blow to the guilty and the innocent alike.

Briefly, there were heady days of celebration for the victors. But only in the immediate aftermath did people begin to grasp just how terrible the war had been. As survivors trickled out of camps of death, the world at last witnessed the extent of the evil that had been unleashed, confronted and finally beaten.

Das Kriegsglück wendete sich. Es stellte sich nun nicht mehr die Frage, wer siegen würde, sondern vielmehr, wie lange die Verlierer noch durchhalten konnten. Dorf um Dorf quer durch die Normandie, noch schneller über weite Gebiete Osteuropas hinweg, schoben sich die Kämpfe näher an Berlin heran. Mussolinis großspurige Herrschaft über Italien fand ein schreckliches Ende. Stadt für Stadt und Lager für Lager wurde aus faschistischer Hand befreit.

Partisanen beschleunigten den Prozeß. Sie blieben nicht länger lautlose Geheimorganisationen, die bei Nacht zuschlugen, sondern traten an die Öffentlichkeit, bekannten Farbe und übernahmen immer größere Gebiete ihres Heimatlandes, während die Besatzungstruppen den Rückzug antraten.

Im Fernen Osten begann die Sonne, über dem japanischen Kaiserreich unterzugehen. Die Kämpfe, die dort stattfanden, gehörten zu den erbittertsten des gesamten Krieges – jede Insel wurde zum Schlachtfeld, und beide Seiten erlitten entsetzliche Verluste. Und dann folgten die abschließenden, ungeheuerlichen Atombombenabwürfe, die sowohl den Schuldigen wie den Unschuldigen einen Todesstoß versetzten.

Für einige kurze Tage stürzten sich die Sieger in begeistertes Feiern. Erst dann, als die Nachwehen einsetzten, begannen die Menschen zu erkennen, wie schrecklich dieser Krieg tatsächlich gewesen war. Die vereinzelten Überlebenden der Vernichtungslager führten der Welt endlich das ganze Ausmaß des Bösen vor Augen, das in diesen Jahren entfesselt, bekämpft und schließlich besiegt worden war.

Le tournant de la guerre était franchi. La question n'était plus qui la gagnerait, mais combien de temps les perdants résisteraient encore. Village après village en Normandie, plus rapidement dans les grands espaces de l'Europe de l'Est, les combattants se rapprochaient toujours plus de Berlin. L'arrogant règne de Mussolini en Italie prit fin de façon abominable. Ville après ville, camp après camp, l'Italie était libérée du joug fasciste.

Les partisans accélérèrent le processus. Ils cessèrent d'être silencieux, avec leurs organisations secrètes qui frappaient de nuit. Ils apparurent en plein jour, reconquérant des régions toujours plus étendues de leur patrie sur les troupes d'occupation battant en retraite.

En Extrême-Orient, le soleil commença à décliner sur l'empire japonais. Les combats dans cette région comptèrent parmi les plus acharnés de toute la guerre – chaque île devint un champ de bataille, les pertes des deux côtés furent épouvantables. Ses monstrueuses explosions finales causèrent la mort subite aussi bien des coupables que des innocents.

Bref, ce furent d'enivrantes journées d'allégresse pour les vainqueurs. Mais il fallut en découvrir les séquelles immédiates pour que les gens commencent à réaliser combien la guerre avait été horrible. Lorsque les survivants revinrent des camps de la mort, le monde mesura enfin l'ampleur du mal qui s'était répandu, auquel il avait été confronté et qu'il avait finalement vaincu.

April 1945. Dead and dying prisoners huddled together
in the concentration camp at Nordhausen, Germany,
50 miles west of Leipzig. They were found lying on straw
by members of the American First Army.

April 1945. Tote und sterbende Gefangene liegen
aneinandergekauert auf Stroh im Konzentrationslager
Nordhausen, 80 Kilometer westlich von Leipzig. Sie
wurden von Mitgliedern der 1. US-Armee gefunden.

Avril 1945. Prisonniers morts ou à l'agonie se côtoyant au
camp de concentration de Nordhausen, en Allemagne, à 80
kilomètres à l'ouest de Leipzig. Des membres de la première
armée américaine les ont découverts gisant sur de la paille.

The entrance to
the camp at Terezin.
The slogan above
the gate reads, 'Work
Makes You Free'.

Der Eingang des
Lagers Theresien-
stadt. Am Tor das
berüchtigte Motto
„Arbeit macht frei".

Entrée du camp
de concentration de
Theresienstadt. Le
slogan surmontant
le portail proclame ·
« Le travail rend
libre ».

By the end of the war the Nazis had established dozens of concentration camps in Germany, Poland and Austria, including the so-called 'death camps' – extermination centres designed to kill entire populations. But thousands of prisoners survived.

Bis zum Ende des Krieges hatten die Nazis Dutzende von Konzentrationslagern in Deutschland, Polen und Österreich errichtet, einschließlich der sogenannten „Vernichtungslager" – diese Zentren dienten der Tötung ganzer Bevölkerungsgruppen. Nur einige tausend Gefangene überlebten.

Jusqu'à la fin de la guerre, les nazis avaient édifié des dizaines de camps de concentration en Allemagne, en Pologne et en Autriche, y compris les sinistres « camps de la mort » – des centres d'extermination destinés à éliminer des populations entières, mais des milliers de prisonniers ont survécu.

A death pit at Bergen-Belsen, 1945. Prisoners were usually kept alive for six weeks, though many died of malnutrition or illness during that time. At the end of the six weeks, most survivors were brutally slaughtered.

Ein Massengrab in Bergen-Belsen, 1945. Die Gefangenen wurden in der Regel sechs Wochen am Leben erhalten. Bereits innerhalb dieses kurzen Zeitraums starben viele von ihnen an Unterernährung oder Krankheit. Anschließend wurden die meisten Überlebenden brutal ermordet.

Un charnier à Bergen-Belsen, en 1945. Les prisonniers étaient généralement maintenus en vie pendant six semaines, mais beaucoup succombaient à la malnutrition ou à la maladie. A la fin des six semaines, la plupart des survivants étaient brutalement abattus.

Buchenwald Camp, May 1945. Prisoners were stripped of anything valuable before being led to the gas chambers – that included gold fillings from their teeth, and, in this case, their wedding rings.

Konzentrationslager Buchenwald, Mai 1945. Bevor die Gefangenen in die Gaskammern geführt wurden, mußten sie alle Wertgegenstände abgeben – dazu gehörten auch die Goldfüllungen in ihren Zähnen und, wie hier zu sehen, ihre Eheringe.

Camp de concentration de Buchenwald, en mai 1945. On prenait aux prisonniers tout ce qui avait la moindre valeur avant de les amener dans les chambres à gaz – y compris leurs dents en or et, dans le cas présent, leurs alliances.

German civilians from nearby are forced to witness the horrors of Buchenwald Camp, 1945. The camp, near Weimar in central Germany, was established in the 1930s.

Deutsche Zivilisten aus der Umgebung werden 1945 von den Alliierten gezwungen, sich das Grauen des Konzentrationslagers Buchenwald anzusehen. Das Lager in der Nähe von Weimar war in den dreißiger Jahren errichtet worden.

Des civils allemands du voisinage sont contraints à venir découvrir les horreurs du camp de Buchenwald, en 1945. Le camp proche de Weimar, dans le centre de l'Allemagne, avait été construit dans les années trente.

German civilians were taken to the death camps immediately after liberation.
They were shown, together with the rest of the world, how the prisoners met
their deaths, how their corpses were transported, and how they were buried.

Unmittelbar nach der Befreiung wurden deutsche Zivilisten in die Konzentrationslager geführt. Man zeigte ihnen und der übrigen Welt, wie die
Gefangenen ums Leben kamen, wie ihre Leichen transportiert wurden und
wie sie begraben wurden.

Des civils allemands sont amenés aux camps de la mort immédiatement
après la libération. On leur montre, ainsi qu'au reste du monde, comment les
prisonniers trouvaient le mort, comment leurs corps étaient transportés et
comment ils étaient enterrés.

May 1945. American editors and publishers witness the horrors of Dachau Camp. The group includes Norman Chandler (*LA Times*), Julius Adler (*NY Times*), M E Walker (*Houston Chronicle*), William Nichols (*This Week*), E Z Dimitman (*Chicago Sun*), William Chenery (*Colliers*) and L K Nicholson (*NO Times*)

Mai 1945. Amerikanische Herausgeber und Verleger werden Zeugen der Schrecken des Konzentrationslagers Dachau. Der Gruppe gehören u. a. Norman Chandler (*LA Times*), Julius Adler (*NY Times*), M. E. Walker (*Houston Chronicle*), William Nichols (*This Week*), E. Z. Dimitman (*Chicago Sun*), William Chenery (*Colliers*) und L. K. Nicholson (*NO Times*) an.

Mai 1945. Des éditeurs et journalistes américains sont témoins de l'horreur à Dachau. Le groupe comprend Norman Chandler (*LA Times*), Julius Adler (*NY Times*), M. E. Walker (*Houston Chronicle*), William Nichols (*This Week*), E. Z. Dimitman (*Chicago Sun*), William Chenery (*Colliers*) et L. K. Nicholson (*NO Times*).

As Allied armies advanced deeper into mainland Europe, partisan groups emerged from the woods and mountains to reclaim their own cities. Here an Italian group associated with the Partito d'Azione patrol the streets of Milan early in 1945.

Während die Armeen der Alliierten tiefer nach Mitteleuropa vordrangen, versuchten Partisanengruppen aus den Wäldern und Bergen, ihre Städte wieder selbst in Besitz zu nehmen. Hier sieht man, wie Anfang 1945 eine italienische Gruppierung, die der Partito d'Azione nahestand, durch die Straßen von Mailand patrouilliert.

Au fur et à mesure que les armées alliées progressent au cœur de l'Europe, des groupes de partisans surgissent des forêts et des montagnes pour revendiquer leur propre ville. Ici, début 1945, un groupe d'Italiens inféodés au Partito d'Azione patrouille dans les rues de Milan.

June 1944. A French Resistance fighter in Chateaudun holds a gun designed by the Czechs and supplied by the British.

Juni 1944. Ein französischer Widerstandskämpfer in Chateaudun trägt ein Gewehr, das in der Tschechoslowakei entwickelt und in Großbritannien hergestellt worden ist.

Juin 1944. Un résistant français, à Chateaudun, tient en mains un fusil fabriqué en Tchécoslovaquie et parachuté par les Britanniques.

August 1944. Members of the French Resistance mopping up
a Paris street. There were those among the Allies who hoped that
the French would rid the city of German troops on their own.
But there were others who fought to be the first to enter Paris.

August 1944. Mitglieder der Résistance säubern eine Straße
in Paris. Viele Alliierte hofften, daß die Franzosen die Stadt im
Alleingang von deutschen Truppen befreien würden. Andere
wiederum kämpften darum, als erste in Paris einzumarschieren.

Août 1944. Membres de la résistance française nettoyant une rue
de Paris. Certains, parmi les alliés, espéraient que les Français
chasseraient eux-mêmes les troupes allemandes de la ville. Mais
d'autres se sont battus pour entrer les premiers dans Paris.

The day of reckoning, France. A French woman (in dark dress) and man (in white shirt) plead their innocence in front of members of the local Resistance. The couple are accused of spying for the Gestapo. They are unlikely to be shown any mercy.

Der Tag der Abrechnung in Frankreich. Zwei Franzosen, eine Frau (im dunklen Kleid) und ein Mann (im weißen Hemd) beteuern ihre Unschuld vor Mitgliedern der örtlichen Résistance. Das Paar wird der Spionage für die Gestapo beschuldigt. Es ist unwahrscheinlich, daß man Gnade walten läßt.

Le jour de la revanche, France. Une Française (en robe noire) et un Français (en chemise blanche) clament leur innocence devant des membres de la résistance locale. Accusés d'espionnage pour la Gestapo, il est peu probable qu'ils aient bénéficié de clémence.

August 1944. A proud group of French locals escort a German prisoner. The man was a member of the SS who had fallen behind when the German army retreated from Chartres. For him, there may be some mercy, as a prisoner of war.

August 1944. Eine stolze Gruppe französischer Einwohner eskortiert einen deutschen Gefangenen. Der Mann war ein Mitglied der SS, die zurückgefallen war, als die deutsche Armee den Rückzug aus Chartres antrat. Für ihn als Kriegsgefangenen mag es ein gewisses Maß an Gnade geben.

Août 1944. Un groupe de Français rayonnant de fierté escortent un prisonnier allemand, un S. S. qui s'est retrouvé derrière les lignes lorsque l'armée allemande a battu en retraite de Chartres. En tant que prisonnier de guerre, on lui aura sans doute réservé un meilleur sort.

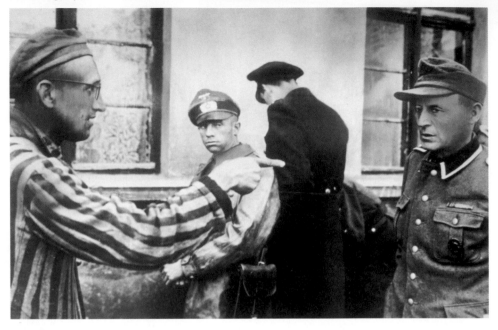

The day of reckoning, Germany. A Russian slave labourer identifies a former Nazi guard and accuses him of brutally beating prisoners. The camp had just been liberated by the American First Army.

Der Tag der Abrechnung in Deutschland. Ein russischer Zwangsarbeiter identifiziert einen früheren Nazi-Aufseher und beschuldigt ihn, Gefangene brutal geschlagen zu haben. Das Lager war gerade von der 1. US-Armee befreit worden.

Le jour de la revanche, Allemagne. Un travailleur forcé russe identifie un ancien gardien nazi et l'accuse d'avoir frappé brutalement des prisonniers. Le camp venait d'être libéré par la première armée américaine.

A group of French women, one with her head shorn, are paraded in public shame. They had been accused of collaborating with German occupying troops. Publication of photographs like this led to an outcry, and the humiliation was stopped.

Französische Frauen, eine davon mit geschorenem Kopf, werden öffentlich angeprangert. Man beschuldigte sie der Kollaboration mit deutschen Besatzungssoldaten. Die Veröffentlichung solcher Aufnahmen führte zu Protesten, so daß die Demütigungen eingestellt wurden.

Un groupe de Françaises, dont l'une a la tête rasée, sont exposées à la vindicte publique. Elles sont accusées d'avoir collaboré avec les troupes d'occupation allemandes. La publication de telles photos a suscité l'indignation et on a mis un terme à cette humiliation.

A German prisoner
of war hurries
through a street in
Toulon, France,
on his way to camp.
The following
jeep will probably
ensure he arrives
bruised but alive.

Ein deutscher
Kriegsgefangener
läuft auf seinem Weg
ins Lager durch eine
Straße im fran-
zösischen Toulon.
Der nachfolgende
Jeep soll dafür
sorgen, daß er –
wenn auch mit
blauen Flecken –
lebendig dort
eintrifft.

Un prisonnier de
guerre allemand
court dans une rue
de Toulon, en
France, pour
rejoindre le camp.
La Jeep qui le suit
doit probablement
garantir qu'il arrive
à destination épuisé,
mais vivant.

A final reckoning.
A young Frenchman,
found guilty
of treason, is tied
to a stake before
execution.

Eine letzte Abrech-
nung. Ein junger
Franzose, schuldig
des Verrats, wird
vor der Exekution
an einen Pfosten
gebunden.

Vengeance finale.
Un jeune Français
accusé de trahison
est attaché à un
poteau avant d'être
exécuté.

In the little village of Sainte-Mère l'Eglise, two miles from the
landing stage of Utah Beach, an elderly Frenchwoman welcomes
an American military policeman to what is left of her home.

In dem kleinen Dorf Sainte-Mère l'Eglise, drei Kilometer
von der Landungsbrücke von Utah Beach entfernt, heißt eine
betagte Französin einen amerikanischen Militärpolizisten in
den Ruinen ihres Hauses willkommen.

Dans le petit village de Sainte-Mère-l'Eglise, à quatre kilomètres
de la plage du débarquement de Utah Beach, une vieille
Française accueille un membre de la police militaire américaine
devant les ruines de sa maison.

August 1944. A member of General Leclerc's Second French Armoured Division, the first Allied troops to enter Paris, leads German prisoners past the Arc de Triomphe. The Tricolour flies once more.

August 1944. Ein Mitglied aus General Leclercs 2. Französischer Panzerdivision, die als erste Truppe der Alliierten in Paris einmarschierte, führt deutsche Gefangene am Triumphbogen vorbei. Die Trikolore weht wieder.

Août 1944. Un membre de la Deuxième division blindée française du général Leclerc, les premières troupes alliées qui entrèrent dans Paris, fait traverser l'Arc de triomphe à des prisonniers allemands. Le drapeau tricolore flotte à nouveau sur la capitale.

Ecstatic Parisians crowd the streets to
cheer American troops, August 1944.
Perhaps, in the long run, it didn't matter
too much which troops liberated Paris.

Ekstatische Pariser Bürger drängen sich
im August 1944 in den Straßen, um
amerikanischen Soldaten zuzujubeln.
Auf lange Sicht machte es keinen allzu
großen Unterschied, welche der Truppen
Paris befreite.

Les Parisiens en liesse envahissent les rues
pour accueillir les troupes américaines,
en août 1944. Sans doute n'est-il pas très
important, à quelques années de distance,
de savoir quelles troupes ont libéré Paris.

German stragglers and sympathizers were still active in the early days of the liberation of Paris. The city was not yet a safe place. French gendarmes and civilians take cover as a sniper fires down into the street.

Deutsche Versprengte und Sympathisanten waren in den ersten Tagen der Befreiung von Paris noch immer aktiv. Die Stadt war noch kein sicherer Ort. Französische Gendarmen und Zivilisten gehen in Deckung, als ein Heckenschütze in die Straße hinunterschießt.

Des francs-tireurs allemands et des sympathisants ont encore sévi durant les premiers jours après la libération de Paris. La ville n'était toujours pas un endroit sûr. Des gendarmes et civils français se mettent à l'abri lorsqu'un franc-tireur tire sur les passants.

The calm after the storm. Soviet troops chat to local
women somewhere in Germany, 1945. The scene is
peaceful and friendly. Perhaps they were all as conscious
of the camera as the young soldier on the left.

Die Ruhe nach dem Sturm. Sowjetische Soldaten unterhalten sich 1945 mit einheimischen Frauen irgendwo in
Deutschland. Die Szene wirkt friedlich und freundlich.
Möglicherweise waren sich alle Beteiligten der Kamera
so bewußt wie der junge Soldat zur Linken.

Le calme après la tempête. Soldats soviétiques
bavardant avec des femmes quelque part en Allemagne,
en 1945. La scène est pacifique et amicale. Peut-être
étaient-ils tous aussi impressionnés par l'appareil photo
que le jeune soldat à gauche au premier plan.

London, July 1944. In the West End, special clubs were set
aside for the use of black US troops. This was at the request of
the American authorities. It did not occur to the majority
of Londoners, at this time, that black and white should be
segregated.

London, Juli 1944. Im West End gab es auf ausdrücklichen
Wunsch der amerikanischen Behörden besondere Clubs für
schwarze US-Soldaten. Den meisten Londoner Bürgern kam zu
dieser Zeit eine Rassentrennung in Schwarze und Weiße nicht in
den Sinn.

Londres, juillet 1944. Dans le West End, des clubs spéciaux ont
été créés, à la demande des autorités américaines, pour les soldats
noirs américains. Il ne serait jamais venu à l'idée de la majorité
des Londoniens de cette époque de séparer les noirs des blancs.

Piccadilly Circus,
December 1942.
American troops
play free pinball
machines at
the American Red
Cross Club.

Piccadilly Circus,
Dezember 1942.
Amerikanische
Soldaten spielen an
Flipperautomaten
im Club des
amerikanischen
Roten Kreuzes.

Piccadilly Circus,
décembre 1942.
Soldats américains
jouant au flipper au
club de la Croix-
Rouge américaine.

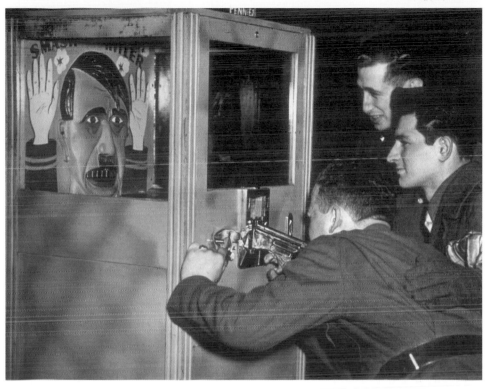

The Club was known as Rainbow Corner. It was an attempt to bring a touch of the United States to troops thousands of miles from home. Prizes for playing the machines were hardly on a Las Vegas scale. The best you could get was a pack of cigarettes.

Dieser Club war bekannt unter dem Namen Rainbow Corner und sollte den Tausende Kilometer von der Heimat entfernten Soldaten ein wenig Amerika Atmosphäre bieten. Die Preise, die beim Glücksspiel gewonnen werden konnten, waren kaum mit denen in Las Vegas zu vergleichen: Der Hauptgewinn war eine Packung Zigaretten.

Le club était connu sous le nom de Rainbow Corner. On voulait ainsi donner aux soldats se trouvant à des milliers de kilomètres de chez eux l'impression qu'ils étaient aux États-Unis. Les prix gagnés en jouant avec les machines n'étaient pas comparables à ceux de Las Vegas. Dans le meilleur des cas, on gagnait un paquet de cigarettes.

The noble art of fraternization. Once the fighting stopped, it wasn't long before
Allied troops began 'fratting', as here in a wood on the outskirts of Berlin. The soldiers
were far from home, and a generation of German men had perished in the war.

Die edle Kunst der Verbrüderung. Nachdem der Krieg vorüber war, ließ das „Fraterni-
sieren" nicht lange auf sich warten – so wie hier in einem Wäldchen am Stadtrand von
Berlin. Die alliierten Soldaten waren fern der Heimat, und eine Generation deutscher
Männer war im Krieg gefallen.

L'art noble de la fraternisation. Une fois les hostilités terminées, il n'a pas fallu
longtemps aux soldats alliés pour commencer à « fraterniser » comme ici, dans une
forêt des environs de Berlin. Les soldats étaient loin de chez eux et toute une
génération d'hommes allemands avait péri durant la guerre.

Although frowned upon by some, the often short-lived romances between Allied troops and German women helped momentarily to relieve some of the bitterness of six long years.

Obwohl sie von manchen mißbilligt wurden, trugen die oft nur kurzlebigen Romanzen zwischen alliierten Soldaten und deutschen Frauen zusehends dazu bei, einen Teil der Bitterkeit abzubauen, die sechs lange Jahre geherrscht hatte.

Bien que critiquées par certains, les romances souvent éphémères entre soldats alliés et Allemandes aidèrent momentanément à oublier l'amertume de six années de guerre.

German soldiers are rounded up by American
troops on the streets of Aachen. The war
in all its misery had come home to Germany.

Amerikanische Truppen stellen in den
Straßen von Aachen deutsche Soldaten.
Der Krieg mit all seinem Elend war nach
Deutschland heimgekehrt.

Soldats allemands rassemblés par les troupes
américaines dans les rues d'Aix-la-Chapelle.
La guerre avec toutes ses horreurs était entrée
sur le territoire de l'Allemagne.

An international misunderstanding: the Russian soldier believes the
woman's bicycle was for sale. It isn't. She struggles to keep this precious
belonging. It happened in Berlin. It could have been in any German city.

Ein internationales Mißverständnis: Der russische Soldat meint, das Fahrrad
der Frau sei zum Kauf angeboten. Das ist es aber nicht, und sie kämpft
darum, diesen wertvollen Besitz zu behalten. So geschehen in Berlin, doch
es hätte auch in jeder anderen deutschen Stadt passieren können.

Malentendu international : le soldat russe croit que la bicyclette de cette
femme est à vendre. Il n'en est rien. Elle se bat pour garder son précieux
bien. La scène se passe à Berlin, mais elle pourrait aussi bien se produire
dans une autre ville allemande.

The Victory Two-Step. Russian and American troops dance together after their respective armies meet in a German town. Within a few years the same soldiers could have been facing each other on either side of the Iron Curtain.

Der Sieges-Twostep. Russische und amerikanische Soldaten tanzen miteinander, als sich ihre Einheiten in einer deutschen Stadt treffen. Wenige Jahre später hätten sich dieselben Soldaten zu beiden Seiten des Eisernen Vorhangs gegenüberstehen können.

Le pas de deux de la victoire. Un soldat russe dansant avec un soldat américain après la jonction de leurs deux armées dans une ville d'Allemagne. Dans quelques années, les mêmes soldats se feront face des deux côtés du rideau de fer.

An historic handshake on 27 April 1945. Infantrymen of the
American First Army meet Soviet soldiers on the remains of the bridge
over the Elbe at Torgau, near Leipzig. Hitler had three days to live.

Ein historischer Handschlag am 27. April 1945. Infanteristen der
1. US-Armee treffen sowjetische Soldaten auf den Überresten der
Elbebrücke bei Torgau, nahe Leipzig. Hitler hatte noch drei Tage zu
leben.

Une poignée de main historique, le 27 avril 1945. Des fantassins de
la première armée américaine rencontrent des soldats soviétiques sur
les vestiges du pont franchissant l'Elbe à Torgau, près de Leipzig.
Hitler n'avait plus que trois jours à vivre.

Perhaps the most famous
picture ever taken by Russian
photographer Yevgeny
Khaldei. It was taken on 30
April 1945, the day Hitler
committed suicide, and shows
the Red Flag being hoisted by
Russian soldiers over the ruins
of the Reichstag in Berlin.

Das wohl berühmteste Foto,
das der russische Fotograf
Jewgeni Khaldei je machte.
Es wurde am 30. April 1945
aufgenommen, dem Tag,
an dem Hitler Selbstmord
verübte, und zeigt, wie
russische Soldaten die Rote
Fahne über der Ruine des
Reichstags in Berlin hissen.

Sans doute la plus célèbre
photo du photographe russe
Yevgeny Khaldei. Elle a été
prise le 30 avril 1945, le jour
où Hitler s'est suicidé, et
représente des soldats russes
hissant le drapeau rouge
sur les ruines du Reichstag à
Berlin.

US paratroopers display a Nazi flag captured in an assault on a French village, not long after the D-day landings. The creases on the flag suggest that it has already been carefully folded and kept in a trooper's backpack. Its destination is certainly the United States.

Amerikanische Fallschirmjäger zeigen eine Nazi-Fahne, die sie bei einem Angriff auf ein französisches Dorf kurz nach dem Tag X eroberten. Die Falten der Fahne lassen vermuten, daß sie schon sorgfältig zusammengelegt in einem der Rucksäcke verstaut worden war. Ihr Bestimmungsort ist sicherlich die Vereinigten Staaten.

Parachutiste américain déployant un drapeau nazi saisi lors de l'assaut d'un village français, quelques jours après le Jour J. Les plis du drapeau indiquent qu'il avait déjà été soigneusement rangé et transporté dans le sac à dos d'un soldat. Il sera certainement emmené aux Etats-Unis.

Meanwhile in the Pacific, other American troops hold a bullet-torn Japanese flag, captured at Eniwetok in the Marshall Islands.

Unterdessen halten andere amerikanische Soldaten im Pazifik eine zerschossene japanische Flagge, die sie in Eniwetok auf den Marshall-Inseln eroberten.

Pendant ce temps, dans le Pacifique, d'autres soldats américains brandissent un drapeau japonais perforé par les balles et conquis à Eniwetok, dans les îles Marshall.

The mixed fortunes of war: Allied victories. American troops
escort Japanese prisoners from the front line as the US forces drive
back the enemy, advancing island by island across the Pacific.

Das Auf und Ab des Krieges: Siege der Alliierten. Amerikanische
Soldaten führen japanische Gefangene von der Frontlinie weg,
während die US-Streitkräfte den Feind zurückdrängen und Insel
für Insel über den Pazifik vorstoßen.

Les diverses fortunes de la guerre : victoires alliées. Des soldats
américains escortent les prisonniers japonais depuis la ligne
de front tandis que les forces américaines repoussent l'ennemi,
avançant d'île en île à travers le Pacifique.

Allied defeats. In the same theatre of war, just a year or two earlier, American and Philippine troops surrender to the Japanese on the island of Bataan.

Niederlagen der Alliierten. Nur ein oder zwei Jahre früher ergeben sich am selben Kriegs-schauplatz amerikanische und philip-pinische Soldaten den Japanern auf der Insel Bataan.

Défaites alliées. Sur le même théâtre de guerre, tout juste un an ou deux plus tôt, des soldats américains et philippins se rendent aux Japonais sur l'île de Bataan.

Chinese soldiers
guard a Japanese
prisoner at Changteh
in the province
of Hunan, 1944.

Chinesische Soldaten
bewachen 1944
einen japanischen
Gefangenen in
Changteh in der
Provinz Hunan.

Soldats chinois
gardant un
prisonnier japonais
à Changteh, dans
la province de
Hunan, en 1944.

After the flag was raised on the Japanese island of Iwo Jima,
American troops surround Japanese soldiers taken prisoner. It took
four days of bitter fighting for the Americans to gain control.

Nachdem sie ihre Flagge auf der japanischen Insel Iwo Jima
gehißt haben, umstellen amerikanische Truppen die gefangenen
japanischen Soldaten. Die Amerikaner benötigten vier Tage
erbitterter Kämpfe, um die Oberhand zu gewinnen.

Après que le drapeau eut été hissé sur l'île japonaise d'Iwo Jima,
des soldats américains regroupent des soldats japonais faits
prisonniers. Il a fallu quatre jours de combats acharnés aux
Américains pour contrôler l'île.

10 August 1945. The day the Japanese offered to surrender.
American troops and a British Wren (Women's Royal Navy Service)
cheer a member of the Chinese Military Mission in Piccadilly Circus.

10. August 1945. Der Tag, an dem die Japaner kapitulierten.
Amerikanische Soldaten und ein weibliches Mitglied der britischen
Marine, eine Wren (Women's Royal Navy Service), lassen einen
chinesischen Militärgesandten im Piccadilly Circus hochleben.

10 août 1945. Le jour où les Japonais ont capitulé. Des soldats
américains et une Wren (Women's Royal Navy Service) britannique
accueillent un membre de la Mission militaire chinoise à Piccadilly
Circus.

On the same day in the same city, a group of Chinese waiters read
the news of Japan's surrender. The two-finger 'Victory V' sign has
been reversed, but it is no doubt intended as a gesture of celebration.

Am gleichen Tag, in der gleichen Stadt, liest eine Gruppe chinesi-
scher Kellner die Nachricht über die Kapitulation Japans. Das mit
zwei Fingern gebildete Siegeszeichen „V" ist zwar verdreht, aber
zweifellos als Geste des Jubels gemeint.

Le même jour dans la même ville, un groupe de serveurs chinois
lisant les nouvelles de la reddition du Japon. Les deux doigts
symbolisant le V de la victoire ont été inversés, mais il s'agit sans
aucun doute d'un geste d'allégresse.

Loudspeakers are
fitted in Trafalgar
Square for a victory
speech by King
George VI. May
brought the end of
the war in Europe,
but Churchill
warned that there
was still a war to be
won in the east.

Auf dem Trafalgar
Square werden für
eine Siegesansprache
König Georgs VI.
Lautsprecher
aufgestellt. Der Mai
brachte das Kriegs-
ende für Europa,
Churchill warnte
jedoch, daß es
immer noch einen
Krieg im Osten zu
gewinnen galt.

Montage de haut-
parleurs, à Trafalgar
Square, pour le
discours de la
victoire du roi
George VI. Le mois
de mai marqua la fin
de la guerre en
Europe, mais
Churchill rappela
qu'il y avait encore
une guerre à gagner
à l'Est.

Three months later came the big parade. Hundreds of thousands swarm over and around the Victoria Monument in London waiting for the appearance of the Royal family on the balcony of Buckingham Palace, 10 August 1945.

Drei Monate später folgte die große Parade. Am 10. August 1945 schwärmen Hunderttausende zum Londoner Denkmal Königin Viktorias und warten darauf, daß die königliche Familie auf dem Balkon von Buckingham Palace erscheint.

Trois mois plus tard, la grande parade. Des centaines de milliers de personnes encerclent le monument de la reine Victoria, à Londres, en attendant que la famille royale apparaisse sur le balcon de Buckingham Palace, le 10 août 1945.

It must be true, it's
in the paper. A lone
GI reads news of
the Nazi surrender,
7 May 1945.

Es steht in der
Zeitung, also muß es
stimmen. Ein GI
liest am 7. Mai 1945
die Nachricht über
die Kapitulation der
Nazis.

C'est certainement
vrai puisque c'est
écrit dans le journal.
Un GI solitaire
lit un article sur la
reddition nazie,
le 7 mai 1945.

Good news travels fast. Jubilant US servicemen
prepare to celebrate in New York, 30 April 1945.
The end of the war in Europe was only a week away.

Gute Nachrichten verbreiten sich schnell.
Triumphierende amerikanische Militärangehörige in
New York stellen sich am 30. April 1945 auf
Siegesfeiern ein. Das Kriegsende in Europa war nur
noch eine Woche entfernt.

Les bonnes nouvelles vont vite. Des militaires
américains ravis s'apprêtent à faire la fête à New
York, le 30 avril 1945. La fin de la guerre en Europe
fut scellée une semaine plus tard seulement.

Children who survived the atom bomb attack on Hiroshima. They are wearing masks to combat the odour of death hanging over the flattened city.

Kinder, die den Atombombenangriff auf Hiroshima überlebten. Sie tragen Masken, um den Geruch des Todes zu bekämpfen, der über der zerstörten Stadt hängt.

Enfants ayant survécu à la bombe atomique d'Hiroshima. Ils portent des masques contre l'odeur de mort qui plane sur la ville martyre.

6 August 1945.
A mushroom-shaped
cloud marks the
destruction of
Hiroshima, and the
first wartime use of
an atomic bomb.

6. August 1945.
Eine pilzförmige
Wolke kennzeichnet
die Zerstörung von
Hiroshima und den
ersten Kriegseinsatz
einer Atombombe.

6 août 1945.
Un nuage en forme
de champignon
symbolise la
destruction
d'Hiroshima et le
premier lancement
d'une bombe
atomique en temps
de guerre.

The last great age of London street parties, May 1945. Children, mothers, grannies – and
a few dads and grandads – pose for the camera at a Victory tea party in Brockley, south-east
London. Weeks earlier a V2 flying bomb had killed dozens of children less than a mile away.

Die letzte große Ära der Londoner Straßenparties, Mai 1945. Kinder, Mütter, Großmütter –
und ein paar Väter und Großväter – posieren in Brockley, Südost-London, bei einer Siegesfeier. Etwa einen Kilometer von hier entfernt hatte wenige Wochen zuvor ein V-2-Geschoß
Dutzende von Kindern getötet.

La dernière grande époque des fêtes des rues à Londres, mai 1945. Enfants, mères, nurses –
et quelques pères et grands-pères – tous posent pour le photographe au thé d'apparat de la
victoire, à Brockley, au sud-est de Londres. Quelques semaines plus tôt, une bombe volante
V2 avait tué des dizaines d'enfants à un peu plus d'un kilomètre de là.

The 'V' motif gathered momentum towards the end of the war. It had been the call sign for resistance groups in Europe. It had become Churchill's trademark. Here three American soldiers have adopted it as their hairstyle.

Das „V"-Motiv wurde gegen Ende des Krieges immer beliebter. Es war das Erkennungszeichen der Widerstandskämpfer in Europa gewesen und zu Churchills Markenzeichen geworden. Hier haben drei amerikanische Soldaten das Motiv als Frisur

Le « V » devint très à la mode vers la fin de la guerre. Signe de reconnaissance des groupes de résistants en Europe, il devint « l'estampille » de Churchill. Ici, ces trois soldats américains l'ont adopté comme coiffure.

Prague welcomes what many later
regarded as a new oppressor. Soviet
marshal Ivan Stepanovich Konev
arrives with a column of Soviet troops,
May 1945. A few months later a
British army officer was to write of
an 'Iron Curtain across Europe'.
Churchill later borrowed the phrase.

Prager Bürger heißen einen Mann
willkommen, den viele später als
neuen Unterdrücker ansahen. Der
sowjetische Marschall Iwan Stepano-
witsch Konew fährt im Mai 1945 mit
einer Kolonne sowjetischer Soldaten in
der Stadt ein. Einige Monate darauf
sollte ein Offizier der britischen Armee
über einen „Eisernen Vorhang quer
durch Europa" schreiben. Churchill
entlehnte später diesen Begriff.

Prague accueille ceux que l'on allait
considérer quelques années plus tard
comme les nouveaux oppresseurs. Le
maréchal soviétique Ivan Stepanovich
Konev arrive avec une colonne de
soldats soviétiques, en mai 1945.
Quelques mois plus tard, un officier
de l'armée britannique écrivit au sujet
d'un « rideau de fer qui s'était abattu
sur l'Europe ». Churchill reprit plus
tard cette phrase.

It's all over! Troops and civilians crowd together in
Piccadilly to celebrate the end of the war in Japan,
15 August 1945. There were some who felt relief rather
than elation. And for many the end had come too late.

Es ist alles vorbei! Soldaten und Zivilisten drängen sich
am 15. August 1945 im Piccadilly, um das Kriegsende in
Japan zu feiern. Manche fühlten eher Erleichterung als
Jubel – für viele war das Kriegsende zu spät gekommen.

C'est fini ! Militaires et civils agglutinés à Piccadilly pour
célébrer la fin de la guerre au Japon, le 15 août 1945.
Pour certains, le soulagement l'emportait sur l'exaltation.
Et, pour beaucoup, la guerre prenait fin trop tard.

For the majority, whether combatants or civilians, the end of the fighting brought a great surge of joy and hope.

Für die Mehrzahl der Menschen, ob Soldaten oder Zivilisten, brachte das Ende des Krieges eine große Welle der Freude und Hoffnung.

Pour la plupart des gens, soldats ou civils, la fin des hostilités fut une profonde source de joie et d'espoir.

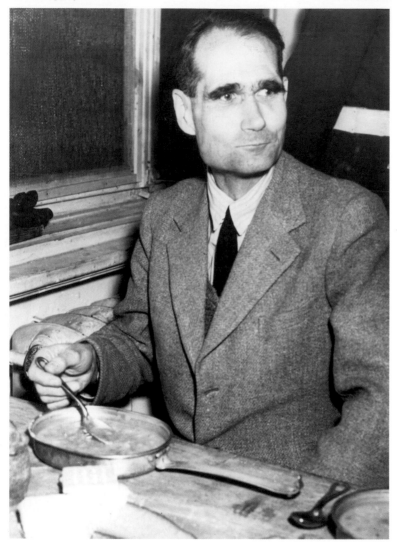

Rudolf Hess,
formerly Hitler's
deputy. Hess died in
prison 41 years later,
having tried to kill
himself four times.

Rudolf Heß, der
ehemalige Stellver-
treter Hitlers. Heß
starb 41 Jahre später
im Gefängnis, nach-
dem er viermal
versucht hatte, sich
umzubringen.

Rudolf Hess,
l'ancien bras droit de
Hitler. Hess est mort
en prison 41 ans
plus tard, après avoir
tenté de se suicider à
quatre reprises.

The Nuremberg Trials. Hermann Goering needed only one suicide attempt. He took cyanide just hours before the time fixed for his execution.

Die Nürnberger Prozesse. Hermann Göring starb beim ersten Selbstmordversuch. Er nahm wenige Stunden vor seiner Exekution Zyanid.

Procès de Nuremberg. Hermann Goering n'a tenté qu'une seule fois de se suicider. Il avala une capsule de cyanure quelques heures seulement avant son exécution.

Two elderly Berliners rest on a bench marked 'Not for Jews', shortly after the end of the war. For them the misery of defeat was not a new experience, but rebuilding their lives would be almost beyond their capabilities.

Zwei betagte Berliner sitzen kurz nach Kriegsende auf einer Bank mit der Aufschrift „Nicht für Juden". Für sie war das Elend einer Niederlage keine neue Erfahrung, doch ihr Leben wieder neu aufzubauen, überstieg fast ihre Kräfte.

Deux vieux Berlinois se reposent sur un banc où est inscrit « Interdit aux juifs », peu de temps après la fin de la guerre. Pour eux, la misère de la défaite n'était pas une expérience nouvelle, mais se reconstruire une nouvelle vie allait être au-dessus de leurs forces.

December 1945.
A young orphan
tries to sell his
father's Iron Cross
for the price of a
few cigarettes.

Dezember 1945.
Ein Waisenjunge
versucht, das Eiserne
Kreuz seines
Vaters zum Preis
einiger Zigaretten
zu verkaufen.

Décembre 1945.
Un jeune orphelin
tente d'échanger la
croix de fer de son
père contre quelques
cigarettes.

# 5. Back to normal
# Zurück zur Normalität
# Retour à la normale

The immense task that lay ahead, March 1946. Just over a year after
the horrific bombing raid, leading citizens of Dresden plan their
new city: (from left to right) Heinz Grünewald (Propaganda Director),
Walter Weidauer (Mayor), and Dr C Herbert (Town Architect).

Eine gewaltige Aufgabe lag im März 1946 vor ihnen. Knapp über
ein Jahr nach dem schrecklichen Bombenangriff auf Dresden planen
führende Bürger ihre neue Stadt (von links nach rechts): Heinz
Grünewald (Propagandaleiter), Walter Weidauer (Bürgermeister) und
Dr. C. Herbert (Stadtbauleiter).

Une tâche immense restait à accomplir, en mars 1946. A peine un an
après l'horrible bombardement aérien, d'éminents citoyens de Dresde
travaillent à la reconstruction de leur ville : (de gauche à droite) Heinz
Grünewald (directeur de la propagande), Walter Weidauer (maire) et
Dr. C. Herbert (architecte municipal).

# 5. Back to normal
# Zurück zur Normalität
# Retour à la normale

Gas masks were thrown away. Bananas and oranges reappeared. Bomb sites became playgrounds. You still couldn't get all the bread, meat, butter, petrol and clothes that you wanted, but at least your sleep was no longer shattered by the air raid siren at night or the bugler's reveille at daybreak.

In Europe there was a massive shortage of houses. Most German cities lay in ruins. Poland was a wasteland. Large areas of the Netherlands, France, Belgium and Britain had been flattened, though not as horrifically as Hiroshima and Nagasaki. As soon as gas, water and electricity supplies had been restored, however, and the streets cleared of rubble, people began to rebuild their lives and their homes.

It was the era of the spiv and the black marketeer – the shifty guy who could get you eggs, petrol coupons, car tyres, nylon stockings, whatever you wanted – at a price. A few made a fortune. Many came to grief. Most made a precarious living.

The promise was that a brand new world would be created – better hospitals, schools, work conditions, and no more unemployment, no more 'us' and 'them'. It nearly happened. But, somehow, what had seemed so simple as an idea became unattainable in practice.

Die Gasmasken wanderten auf den Müll. Es gab wieder Bananen und Apfelsinen. Trümmer-grundstücke wurden als Spielplätze genutzt. Zwar waren Brot, Fleisch, Butter, Benzin und Kleidung noch immer rationiert, aber dafür wurde wenigstens der Schlaf nicht mehr von Sire-nen gestört, die Fliegeralarm meldeten, oder vom Wecksignal des Hornisten bei Tagesanbruch.

In Europa herrschte enormer Wohnungsmangel. Die meisten deutschen Städte lagen in Schutt und Asche. Polen glich einer Wüstenei. Große Gebiete in den Niederlanden, Frankreich, Belgien und Großbritannien waren dem Erdboden gleichgemacht worden, wenn auch nicht auf die gleiche schreckliche Art wie Hiroshima und Nagasaki. Sobald die Gas-, Wasser- und Stromversorgung wiederhergestellt war und die Trümmer von den Straßen geräumt waren, begannen die Menschen damit, ihr Leben und ihre Häuser wieder aufzubauen.

Es war die Ära der schmierigen Typen und Schwarzmarkthändler, der gerissenen Burschen, die Eier, Benzingutscheine, Autoreifen, Nylonstrümpfe oder was auch immer besorgen konnten – allerdings zu gesalzenen Preisen. Manche machten auf diese Weise ein Vermögen. Viele kamen zu Schaden. Die Mehrheit führte ein unsicheres Leben.

Man hatte die Hoffnung, daß eine völlig neue Welt geschaffen würde – daß es bessere Krankenhäuser, Schulen, Arbeitsbedingungen gäbe und keine Arbeitslosigkeit mehr, kein „wir" und „die da oben". Fast wäre es soweit gekommen. Doch erwies sich das, was als Idee so einfach schien, in der Praxis leider nicht als umsetzbar.

On se débarrassa des masques à gaz tandis que les bananes et les oranges réapparaissaient. Les endroits bombardés servaient de terrains de jeux. On ne pouvait, certes, pas encore trouver tout le pain, la viande, le beurre, le carburant ou les vêtements que l'on désirait, mais, au moins, on n'était plus brutalement arraché à son sommeil, en pleine nuit, par la sirène d'alerte d'un raid aérien ou le son du clairon au petit matin.

En Europe, la pénurie de logements était dramatique. La plupart des villes allemandes étaient en ruine. La Pologne était un véritable désert. Des régions entières des Pays-Bas, de France, de Belgique et de Grande-Bretagne avaient été détruites, de façon certes moins horribles qu'à Hiroshima et Nagasaki. Mais, dès que le gaz, l'eau et le courant furent rétablis et que les rues furent vidées de leurs gravats, les gens commencèrent à reconstruire leur vie et leur maison.

Ce fut l'heure des trafiquants et du marché noir – avec les roublards qui pouvaient vous procurer des œufs, des coupons d'essence, des pneus de voiture, des bas en nylon, tout ce que vous vouliez – mais à quel prix! Certains firent fortune, mais pour beaucoup, les choses tournèrent mal. Ils vécurent souvent une vie précaire.

A en croire les promesses, un monde tout neuf allait être créé – de meilleurs hôpitaux, de meilleures écoles, de meilleures conditions de travail, mais plus de chômage, plus de « nous » et « eux ». Cela faillit réussir. Mais, en réalité, ce que l'on avait cru être si simple s'avéra irréalisable dans la pratique.

A Royal Air Force officer tries on a trilby hat from the limited range of 'demob' (demobilization) issue. Leaving the Forces was like joining up in reverse. Gradually the military personality gave way to a civilian one.

Ein Offizier der Royal Air Force probiert einen weichen Filzhut aus dem begrenzten Angebot der „Ausstattung zur Entlassung aus dem Kriegs-dienst". Die Armee zu verlassen, war ähnlich, wie in sie einzutreten, nur im umgekehrten Sinn: Nach und nach wich das militärische Wesen einem bürgerlichen.

Un officier de la Royal Air Force essaie un chapeau mou des stocks limités de la « démob » (démobilisation). Quitter l'armée signifiait un recrutement dans le sens inverse. Peu à peu, les militaires s'effacèrent devant les civils.

March 1944. A rehearsal for the real thing. Demobilization was still 18 months away, but already the Allies were confident that the worst of the war was over. A sergeant takes part in a 'demob' practice at an army demobilization centre, Olympia, London.

März 1944. Eine Probe für den Ernstfall. Bis zur Demobilisierung sollten noch anderthalb Jahre vergehen. Doch schon jetzt waren die Alliierten zuversichtlich, daß die schlimmste Zeit des Krieges hinter ihnen lag. Ein Feldwebel nimmt an einer „demob"-Übung in einem Demobilisierungszentrum in Olympia, London, teil.

Mars 1944. L'étalage de la réalité. La démobilisation remontait à seulement 18 mois, mais les Alliés, déjà, étaient convaincus que la pire des guerres venait de se terminer. Un sergent participe à un test de « démob » dans un centre de démobilisation de l'armée, à l'Olympia, Londres.

GI brides leave Southampton, bound for the United States. Before the war few British women had ever met an American. Now many were embarking on a new life in a new continent. It was just another example of the way the war so dramatically changed people's lives.

GI-Bräute verlassen Southampton, um in die Vereinigten Staaten zu reisen. Vor dem Krieg hatten nur wenige britische Frauen je einen Amerikaner kennengelernt. Nun machten sich viele von ihnen auf, ein neues Leben auf einem neuen Kontinent zu beginnen. Dies ist nur ein weiteres Beispiel dafür, wie sehr der Krieg das Leben der Menschen veränderte.

Des fiancées de GI quittent Southampton en direction des Etats-Unis. Avant la guerre, bien peu de femmes britanniques avaient déjà rencontré un Américain. Maintenant, elles étaient nombreuses à s'embarquer pour une nouvelle vie sur un nouveau continent. Cela illustre à quel point la guerre a modifié dramatiquement la vie des gens.

February 1946. A US Marine is reunited with his GI bride and son, newly arrived in the United States. Not all wartime romances ended so happily. There were broken hearts and broken promises all over Europe.

Februar 1946. Ein amerikanischer Marinesoldat ist wieder mit seiner GI-Braut und seinem Sohn vereint, die gerade in den USA eingetroffen sind. Nicht alle Kriegsromanzen endeten so glücklich. Überall in Europa gab es gebrochene Herzen und gebrochene Versprechen.

Février 1946. Un soldat de la marine américaine retrouve sa fiancée et son fils, tout juste arrivés aux Etats-Unis. Les romances de la guerre n'ont pas toutes en un dénouement aussi heureux. L'Europe entière connut des cœurs brisés et des promesses non tenues.

August 1946.
A prefabricated
house arrives at its
site. Four lorries
could deliver the
entire house.

August 1946. Ein
Fertighaus erreicht
seinem Bestim-
mungsort. Vier
Lastwagen genügten,
um das gesamte
Haus zu liefern.

Août 1946. Une
maison préfabriquée
arrive à destination.
Quatre camions
suffisaient pour
transporter toute
une maison.

Coming back to a new home. Gunner Murdoch arrives at his
'prefab' (prefabricated house) in Tulse Hill, London, to be greeted
by his wife and son. He had been away for four and a half years,
most of which he had spent as a Japanese prisoner of war.

Rückkehr in ein neues Heim. Artillerist Murdoch wird vor
seinem Fertighaus in Tulse Hill, London, von seiner Frau und
seinem Sohn empfangen. Viereinhalb Jahre war er fort gewesen
und hatte den größten Teil der Zeit in japanischer Kriegsge-
fangenschaft verbracht.

De retour dans une nouvelle maison. Le canonnier Murdock
rentre chez lui, dans sa maison préfabriquée de Tulse Hill,
à Londres, où il est accueilli par sa femme et son fils. Absent
pendant quatre ans et demi, il avait passé presque tout ce temps
comme prisonnier de guerre japonais.

March 1946. A taste of peace. Children sample the first
batch of bananas to arrive in Britain after the war.
Jack Marks, the importer, can just be seen in the crowd
(far right, back).

März 1946. Ein Geschmack des Friedens. Kinder
probieren die ersten Bananen, die nach Kriegsende in
Großbritannien eintreffen. Man kann Jack Marks, der
sie importierte, gerade noch in der Menschenmenge
erkennen (ganz rechts, im Hintergrund).

Mars 1946. Le goût de la paix. Des enfants goûtent les
premières bananes arrivées en Grande-Bretagne après la
guerre. On distingue à peine Jack Marks, l'importateur,
derrière le groupe (tout à droite, au fond).

The arrival of such luxuries as bananas was given the same sort of press coverage reserved for film stars or heads of state.

Die Presse bedachte das Eintreffen von Luxusgütern wie Bananen mit einer Berichterstattung, die sonst Filmstars oder Staatsoberhäuptern vorbehalten war.

L'arrivée d'un produit de luxe comme les bananes bénéficia de la même espèce de couverture de presse que celle qu'on réservait aux vedettes de cinéma ou aux chefs d'Etat.

The fight for the beaches is over, 19 August 1944. This picture was taken only two and a half months after D-day.

Der Kampf um die Küste ist vorüber, 19. August 1944. Diese Aufnahme entstand nur zwei-einhalb Monate nach dem Tag X.

La bataille pour les plages est terminée, 19 août 1944. Cette photo a été prise deux mois et demi seulement après le Jour J.

Most British seaside resorts reopened for business before the war ended, but some beaches were still littered with mines, barbed wire and other relics of the invasion scare. This bather seems determined to brave all that and the awful British weather.

Die meisten britischen Seebäder waren schon vor Kriegsende wieder für Besucher geöffnet, obwohl einige Strände noch mit Minen, Stacheldraht und anderen Relikten der Invasionsvorsorge übersät waren. Dieser Badende scheint entschlossen, all diesen Dingen zu trotzen, ebenso wie dem furchtbaren englischen Wetter.

La majorité des stations balnéaires de Grande-Bretagne rouvrirent avant même que la guerre s'achève, mais certaines plages étaient encore infestées de mines, de fil de fer barbelé et autres vestiges de l'invasion. Ce sportif semble déterminé à braver tout cela et le mauvais temps anglais.

February 1947. Families collect their coke rations
from the South Metropolitan Gas Company's depot at
Vauxhall, London. The winter of 1946/47 was one
of the coldest in memory, and 'back to normal' did not
mean back to plenty. All fuel was still rationed.

Februar 1947. Familien holen ihre Koksrationen am
Depot des Süd-Londoner Gaswerks in Vauxhall ab.
Der Winter 1946/47 war einer der kältesten seit
Menschengedenken, und „zurück zur Normalität"
bedeutete nicht etwa „zurück zum Überfluß". Alle
Brennstoffe blieben weiterhin rationiert.

Février 1947. Des familles se procurent leurs rations de
charbon au dépôt de la South Metropolitan Gas
Company, à Vauxhall, Londres. L'hiver 1946/47 a été
l'un des plus froids de mémoire d'homme et « retour à
la normale » ne signifiait pas retour à l'abondance. Tous
les carburants et combustibles étaient encore rationnés.

Canadian soldiers of a field hygiene section delouse Russian prisoners of war recently liberated from a camp near Friesoythe, 30 miles west of Bremen. The Russians had been prisoners for over two years. They would have been infested with lice for almost all that time.

Kanadische Soldaten einer Feldhygiene-Einheit entlausen russische Kriegsgefangene, die kurz zuvor aus einem Lager in der Nähe von Friesoythe, 50 Kilometer westlich von Bremen, befreit worden sind. Die Russen waren über zwei Jahre in Gefangenschaft und wohl fast ebenso lang mit Läusen verseucht.

Soldats canadiens d'une section d'hygiène de campagne désinfectant des prisonniers de guerre russes récemment libérés d'un camp près de Friesoythe, à 50 kilomètres à l'ouest de Brême. Les Russes avaient été en captivité pendant plus des deux ans et sans doute été infestés de poux pendant presque tout ce temps.

April 1948. Nurses from UNICEF (United Nations International Children's Emergency Fund) spray the hair of a young German deportee from Czechoslovakia. The spray is almost certainly DDT, and therefore toxic

April 1948. Eine Krankenschwester des Weltkinderhilfs-werks UNICEF besprüht das Haar eines aus der Tschechoslowakei deportierten deutschen Kindes. Der Sprühnebel ist mit größter Wahr-scheinlichkeit DDT und daher toxisch.

Avril 1948. Des infirmières de l'UNICEF (Fonds des Nations unies pour l'enfance) pulvérisent les cheveux d'une petite déportée allemande de Tchécoslovaquie. Le produit, très certainement du DDT, est donc toxique.

September 1949.
The Berlin airlift
delivers the one
millionth bag of coal
at Gatow Airport,
following the Soviet
Union's blockade of
land routes.

September 1949.
Über die Berliner
Luftbrücke wird der
einmillionste Koh-
lensack auf dem
Flughafen Gatow
angeliefert, nachdem
die Sowjetunion die
Landwege blockiert
hatte.

Septembre 1949.
Le pont aérien de
Berlin achemine le
millionième sac de
charbon à l'aéroport
de Gatow après que
l'Union soviétique
eut bloqué les accès
routiers à Berlin.

A German airlift worker's wife looks after Berlin children as they munch their ration of one slice of bread and margarine. The parcel at the side is from the Red Cross. The Berlin airlift lasted about a year, after the Soviet Union halted all deliveries of food and supplies overland.

Die Frau eines deutschen Luftbrückenmitarbeiters betreut Berliner Kinder, die ihre Ration von einer Scheibe Brot mit Margarine genießen. Das Päckchen auf der Seite stammt vom Roten Kreuz. Etwa ein Jahr lang unterband die Sowjetunion jegliche Lebensmittellieferungen auf dem Landweg. In dieser Zeit bestand die Berliner Luftbrücke.

Une auxiliaire allemande du pont aérien s'occupe d'enfants berlinois mangeant leur ration – une tranche de pain avec de la margarine. Le paquet à sa droite a été envoyé par la Croix-Rouge. Le pont aérien de Berlin a duré environ un an pendant lequel l'Union soviétique interdit tout approvisionnement par voie terrestre en nourriture et autres produits.

The divided city, 1948. This line across Berlin's Potsdamer Straße was to prevent police from the Russian sector pursuing criminals into the Western Zone.

Die geteilte Stadt im Jahre 1948. Diese quer über Berlins Potsdamer Straße verlaufende Linie sollte die Polizei des russischen Sektors daran hindern, Verbrecher in die Westzone hinüber zu verfolgen.

La cité divisée, 1948. Cette ligne à travers la Postdamer Straße de Berlin était censée empêcher la police du secteur russe de poursuivre les criminels dans les secteurs occidentaux.

July 1948.
A displaced person
sells a tin of food to
a Berliner after
hearing that she will
be deported from
the compound at
Mariendorf.

Juli 1948. Eine
Zwangsvertriebene
verkauft eine Dose
Büchsennahrung an
einen Berliner, nach-
dem sie erfahren hat,
daß sie aus dem
Lager in Mariendorf
deportiert werden
wird.

Juillet 1948. Une
personne déplacée
vend une boîte de
conserve à un
Berlinois après avoir
appris qu'elle allait
être transférée du
camp de Marien-
dorf.

July 1945. Poles await distribution of bread and blankets by UNRRA
(United Nations Relief and Rehabilitation Administration) workers at Weimar
Station, Germany. The former occupants of a slave labour camp had opted
not to return to Poland but to travel west to Bavaria to work on farms.

Juli 1945. Polen warten auf Brot und Decken, die Mitarbeiter der UNRRA
(United Nations Relief and Rehabilitation Administration) auf dem Bahnhof
von Weimar verteilen. Die ehemaligen Insassen eines Arbeitslagers hatten sich
dafür entschieden, nicht nach Polen zurückzukehren, sondern in den Westen,
nach Bayern, zu reisen, um dort auf Bauernhöfen zu arbeiten.

Juillet 1945. Polonais attendant la distribution de pain et de couvertures par
des membres de l'UNRRA (Agence des Nations unies pour les secours et la
réhabilitation), à la gare de Weimar, en Allemagne. Les anciens occupants
d'un camp de travaux forcés avaient choisi de ne pas retourner en Pologne,
mais de partir vers l'Ouest pour travailler dans des fermes en Bavière.

July 1947. A Dutch woman kisses her grandchild for the first
time. The barbed wire fence divided the mining town of Kerkrade
in two – one half in Germany, the other in the Netherlands.
It took years before some families were reunited after the war.

Juli 1947. Eine holländische Frau küßt zum ersten Mal ihr
Enkelkind. Der Stacheldrahtzaun teilte die Bergarbeiterstadt
Kerkrade in zwei Teile – die eine Hälfte lag in Deutschland, die
andere in den Niederlanden. Es sollte noch Jahre dauern, bis
manche Familien nach dem Krieg wieder vereint waren.

Juillet 1947. Une Hollandaise embrasse son petit-fils pour la
première fois. La clôture de fil de fer barbelé divise la ville
minière de Kerkrade en deux secteurs, un en Allemagne, l'autre
aux Pays-Bas. Il a fallu attendre des années pour que certaines
familles soient réunies après la guerre.

October 1944. German refugees queue for soup in a former
German army barrack at Brand, near Aachen. The people in the
queue are 'room presidents', each responsible for a section of
refugees. In all, there were 4,500 displaced people in the camp.

Oktober 1944. Deutsche Flüchtlinge stehen nach Suppe an in
einer ehemaligen deutschen Militärkaserne in Brand bei Aachen.
Die Personen in der Schlange sind „Stubenführer", die für jeweils
eine Gruppe von Flüchtlingen verantwortlich waren. In diesem
Lager befanden sich insgesamt 4.500 Zwangsvertriebene.

Octobre 1944. Réfugiés allemands faisant la queue pour manger
dans une ancienne caserne de l'armée allemande à Brand, près
d'Aix-la-Chapelle. Les gens dans la file sont des « présidents
de pièce », chacun étant responsable d'un groupe de réfugiés.
Au total, 4 500 personnes déplacées logeaient dans ce camp.

October 1945.
One of thousands
homeless Germans,
wandering from
East Germany to the
Western Sector
of Berlin, rests for a
while to bathe her
aching feet.

Oktober 1945.
Eine der Tausenden
von obdachlosen
Deutschen, die von
Ostdeutschland in
den Westsektor
Berlins wanderten,
legt eine kurze Pause
ein, um ihre schmer-
zenden Füße zu
kühlen.

Octobre 1945. Une
jeune fille parmi les
milliers d'Allemands
sans domicile durant
leur exode
d'Allemagne de l'Est
vers le secteur
occidental de Berlin,
se reposant un
instant pour laver ses
jambes douloureuses.

May 1945. Frederick Ramage's picture of French, Belgian, Dutch and Polish refugees crossing the Elbe over what is left of the bridge at Tangermünde. The bridge had been blown up by the retreating German army. The refugees are fleeing from the advancing Russians.

Mai 1945. Frederick Ramages Aufnahme zeigt französische, belgische, holländische und polnische Flüchtlinge beim Überqueren der Elbe auf den Überresten der Brücke von Tangermünde. Die Brücke war von der deutschen Wehrmacht auf dem Rückzug gesprengt worden. Die Menschen flüchten vor den heranrückenden Russen.

Mai 1945. Cliché de Frederick Ramage représentant des réfugiés français, belges, hollandais et polonais traversant l'Elbe sur ce qui reste du pont de Tangermünde, miné par l'armée allemande en retraite. Les réfugiés fuient devant les Russes qui se rapprochent.

Another photograph by Frederick Ramage – July 1945. The streets of Berlin have been cleared of rubble. Public transport has been restored, but there is no room on buses or trams for heavy loads. Women use handcarts to pull what few possessions they have left as they search for somewhere to live.

Eine weitere Fotografie von Frederick Ramage – Juli 1945. Die Straßen Berlins sind von Trümmern befreit worden. Öffentliche Verkehrsmittel haben den Transport zwar wieder aufgenommen, es findet sich jedoch in Bussen oder Straßenbahnen kein Platz für umfangreiche Lasten. Frauen benutzen deshalb Handwagen, um die wenige Habe, die ihnen geblieben ist, auf der Suche nach einer neuen Bleibe zu befördern.

Une autre photographie de Frederick Ramage – juillet 1945. Les rues de Berlin ont été débarrassées des gravats. Les transports collectifs recommencent à circuler, mais il n'y a pas de place, dans les bus ou les tramways, pour transporter des fardeaux encombrants. Les femmes chargent sur des carrioles les quelques biens qui leur sont restés et partent à la recherche d'un endroit où s'installer.

Two images of postwar Berlin by Frederick Ramage. Soldiers (left) returning
from the front and homeless civilians gather at a railway terminus, July 1945. Berlin
families (above) pass a Russian poster as they seek a new home, October 1945.

Das Nachkriegs-Berlin in zwei Aufnahmen von Frederick Ramage. Von der Front
zurückkehrende Soldaten und obdachlose Zivilisten (links) versammeln sich in der
Endstation einer Eisenbahnlinie im Juli 1945. Berliner Familien (oben) ziehen auf der
Suche nach einem neuen Heim im Oktober 1945 an einem russischen Plakat vorbei.

Deux photos du Berlin de l'après-guerre par Frederick Ramage. A gauche, des
soldats revenant du front et des civils sans domicile rassemblés au terminus de la
gare de chemin de fer, en juillet 1945. Famille berlinoise (ci-dessus), dépassant une
pancarte russe dans leur recherche d'un nouveau foyer, en octobre 1945.

1949. Groundnuts (peanuts) from East Africa, grown in a government-sponsored initiative, are sucked from the hold of a cargo ship in the London Docks.

1949. Erdnüsse aus Ostafrika, die mit Regierungsgeldern angebaut worden waren, werden aus dem Laderaum eines Frachtschiffs im Londoner Hafen abgesaugt.

1949. Des cacahuètes d'Afrique orientale, fruit d'une initiative lancée par le gouvernement, sont transbordées des cales d'un cargo dans les docks de Londres.

February 1949. The 'European Recovery Program', known as Marshall Aid, brings sugar to the Royal Victoria Docks, London. The scheme began in 1947.

Februar 1949. Das „Europäische Wiederaufbau-Programm", allgemein Marshallplan genannt, bringt Zucker in die Royal Victoria Docks in London. Die Umsetzung des Programms begann 1947.

Février 1949. L'« European Recovery Program », mieux connu sous le nom de Plan Marshall, amène du sucre aux Royal Victoria Docks de Londres. Le projet a débuté en 1947.

January 1947. Two limbless ex-servicemen make artificial limbs
for others maimed by the war. They were taking part in an
exhibition sponsored by the Ministries of Health and Labour.

Januar 1947. Zwei versehrte ehemalige Militärangehörige
stellen Prothesen für andere im Krieg verletzte Menschen her.
Sie nahmen an einer vom Gesundheits- und vom Arbeitsmini-
sterium finanzierten Ausstellung teil.

Janvier 1947. Deux anciens soldats ayant perdu un avant-bras
fabriquent des prothèses pour d'autres handicapés de guerre.
Ils participent à une exposition organisée par les ministères de
la Santé et du Travail.

German production lines roll again, 1947. This is the final operation on the assembly line of a Ford factory. The United States pumped vast economic aid into Germany after the war to prevent Communism creeping ever westwards.

Deutsche Fließbänder laufen wieder, 1947. Am Montageband eines Fordwerks wird abschließend Hand angelegt. Nach dem Krieg flossen aus den Vereinigten Staaten Riesensummen an Wirtschaftshilfe nach Deutschland, um zu verhindern, daß der Kommunismus immer weiter Richtung Westen vordringen würde.

Les chaînes de production allemandes recommencent à tourner en 1947. Ici, il s'agit des dernières opérations sur la chaîne de montage d'une usine Ford. Les Etats-Unis ont fourni une aide économique considérable à l'Allemagne après la guerre pour empêcher le communisme de se propager plus avant à l'Ouest.

Bricklayers working for the Ilford Borough Council, July 1947. 'Homes fit for heroes' had been a slogan and a broken promise after World War I. The Labour Government did more to house people decently after World War II.

Maurer arbeiten für den Bezirksrat von Ilford im Juli 1947. „Heime für Helden" war nach dem Ersten Weltkrieg erst ein bekannter Slogan und dann ein gebrochenes Versprechen geworden. Die Labour-Regierung leistete später mehr, um nach dem Zweiten Weltkrieg die Menschen angemessen unterzubringen.

Maçons travaillant pour l'Ilford Borough Council, juillet 1947. « Des foyers pour les héros »: un slogan et une promesse jamais tenue après la Première Guerre mondiale. Le gouvernement travailliste fit plus pour loger décemment les gens après la Seconde Guerre mondiale.

Dresden, March 1946. Gustav and Alma Piltz help to clear rubble just over a year after the RAF and the USAF reduced their city to a smoking ruin. Two generations later the Allied raids on Dresden are still the subject of much controversy.

Dresden, März 1946. Knapp über ein Jahr nachdem die britische und amerikanische Luftwaffe ihre Stadt in Schutt und Asche gelegt hat, helfen Gustav und Alma Piltz bei der Räumung von Trümmern. Auch zwei Generationen später sind die Angriffe der Alliierten auf Dresden immer noch ein sehr kontrovers diskutiertes Thema.

Dresde, mars 1946. Gustav et Alma Piltz aident à déblayer les gravats un an à peine après que la RAF et l'armée de l'air américaine eurent transformé leur ville en ruines fumantes. Deux générations futures, les raids alliés sur Dresde sont encore le sujet de nombreuses controverses.

Dresden, March 1946. A human chain of women workers move bricks to be used
in the rebuilding of their city. In the background are the remains of the Roman
Catholic cathedral. Until the Allied raid, Dresden had been one of the Baroque
centres of beauty in Europe.

Dresden, März 1946. Frauen bilden eine Kette, um Backsteine für den
Wiederaufbau ihrer Stadt weiterzureichen. Im Hintergrund sieht man die
Überreste eines mächtigen katholischen Kirchenbaus. Bis zum Angriff der
Alliierten galt Dresden als eine der Barock-Hochburgen Europas.

Dresde, mars 1946. Une chaîne humaine d'ouvrières transporte des briques qui
serviront à reconstruire leur ville. A l'arrière-plan, les restes de la cathédrale. Avant
d'être bombardée, Dresde avait été l'une des plus belles villes baroques d'Europe.

In their first summer of peace since 1939, citizens of
Magdeburg queue for water at a pump. It is a scene that could
have been witnessed in almost any German city in 1945.

In ihrem ersten Friedenssommer seit 1939 stehen Einwohner
von Magdeburg Schlange an einer Wasserpumpe. Solch
eine Szene konnte man 1945 in fast jeder deutschen Stadt
beobachten.

Durant le premier été de paix depuis 1939, des citoyens de
Magdebourg font la queue devant la pompe pour obtenir de
l'eau. Cette scène pourrait se passer dans pratiquement toutes
les villes d'Allemagne de 1945.

Just a few months after the beginning of
the Marshall Aid programme, German women
water young trees in a horticultural nursery.

Nur wenige Monate nach Beginn der
Umsetzung des Marshallplans gießen deutsche
Frauen junge Bäume in einer Baumschule.

Quelques mois seulement après l'inauguration
du programme d'aide du Plan Marshall, des
Allemandes arrosent de jeunes arbres dans une
pépinière.

Berliner Straße in the Western Sector of the city, 1948. Self-help complements
Marshall Aid from the USA. The worst of the suffering was over. A year or two
earlier these street allotments would have been ravaged by starving refugees.

Die Berliner Straße im Westsektor der Stadt, 1948. Selbsthilfe ergänzt den
Marshallplan aus den USA. Die schlimmste Zeit des Elends war vorüber. Ein oder
zwei Jahre früher wären diese Straßen-Schrebergärten noch von hungernden
Flüchtlingen geplündert worden.

La Berliner Straße dans le secteur occidental de la ville en 1948. Les initiatives
individuelles viennent compléter le Plan Marshall américain. Le pire était passé. Un an
ou deux plus tôt, ces potagers de rue auraient été pris d'assaut par les réfugiés affamés.

November 1948. A Berlin park has become a wilderness.
For the young, there is nowhere to play. For the elderly, there
is nowhere to sit. The wood from the park benches has been
torn off and taken away to be used for fuel.

November 1948. Ein verwilderter Berliner Park. Für die Kinder
gibt es keinen Platz zum Spielen, für die alten Leute keinen Platz
zum Sitzen. Das Holz der Parkbänke diente als Brennmaterial.

Novembre 1948. Parc berlinois à l'abandon. Pour les enfants, il
n'existe pas de terrains de jeux. Pour les plus âgés, aucun endroit
où s'asseoir. Le bois des bancs du parc a été arraché et a servi de
combustible.

July 1945. An old
woman clears rubble
in the Russian Zone
of Berlin (picture by
Frederick Ramage).

Juli 1945. Eine alte
Frau räumt Trümmer
im russischen Sektor
Berlins (Bild von
Frederick Ramage).

Juillet 1945.
Une vieille femme
déblaye des gravats
dans le secteur russe
de Berlin (photo
prise par Frederick
Ramage).

# 6. New nations, new problems
# Neue Nationen, neue Probleme
# Nouvelles nations, nouveaux problèmes

The homeless come home, the wanderers come to rest. Jewish
refugees arrive at a British camp on their way to Palestine
in 1947, a year in which Zionist terrorism was at its height
and an independent Israel still seemed heartbreaks away.

Die Heimatlosen kehren heim und kommen zur Ruhe.
Jüdische Flüchtlinge bei der Ankunft in einem britischen
Lager, von wo sie 1947 nach Palästina gelangten. In diesem
Jahr befand sich der zionistische Terrorismus auf seinem
Höhepunkt, und ein unabhängiges Israel schien noch um
einiges Leid entfernt zu sein.

Les sans-abri trouvent un domicile, ceux qui sont en route
trouvent le repos. Des réfugiés juifs arrivent dans un camp
britannique dont ils repartiront pour la Palestine en 1947,
une année durant laquelle le terrorisme sioniste atteignit son
apogée et un Israël indépendant sembla rester une utopie.

# 6. New nations, new problems
## Neue Nationen, neue Probleme
## Nouvelles nations, nouveaux problèmes

By the late summer of 1945 millions of bewildered and homeless people were on the move – across Europe and the Far East. They were looking for somewhere to live, and for many of them that meant a new country.

It was a time of change. The old European colonial powers were bankrupt. Imperial futures had been mortgaged to the hilt to raise money for the war. And, to ensure the cooperation of their subjects, the old rulers had made promises that were now being called in. India demanded independence. Muslims in that subcontinent demanded partition. Jews demanded a land of their own. In China, no demand was necessary. The Communists simply took over.

In all these places there was more killing. In its first year, the new state of Israel had to survive a war against five Arab neighbours. But the actual process was sometimes surprisingly easy. Britain left India with scarcely a murmur.

Where possible, the newly established United Nations did what it could to help, establishing camps for refugees, trying to reunite families that had been blown apart by the misfortunes of war. It was a slow and heartbreaking task.

Im Spätsommer des Jahres 1945 waren Millionen orientierungsloser und obdachloser Menschen unterwegs – überall in Europa und auch im Fernen Osten. Sie suchten einen Ort, an dem sie leben konnten. Für viele bedeutete dies ein anderes Land.

Es war eine Zeit des Umbruchs. Die alten europäischen Kolonialmächte waren zahlungsunfähig. Die Zukunft der Weltreiche war bis aufs Mark mit Kriegshypotheken belastet. Außerdem hatten die alten Regenten, um sich der Kooperation ihrer Untertanen zu versichern, Versprechen gegeben, die nun eingefordert wurden. Indien verlangte die Unabhängigkeit. Die Moslems dieses Subkontinents forderten überdies eine Teilung. Die Juden verlangten ein eigenes Land. In China hingegen, war keine Forderung notwendig. Die Kommunisten lösten schlichtweg die Regierung ab.

An all diesen Orten gab es weiteres Blutvergießen. In seinem ersten Jahr war der neugeborene Staat Israel bereits gezwungen, einen Krieg gegen fünf arabische Nachbarn zu überstehen. Neustrukturierungen vollzogen sich dennoch manchmal mit erstaunlicher Leichtigkeit. Großbritannien verließ Indien fast ohne das leiseste Murren.

Wo immer es möglich war, halfen die neugegründeten Vereinten Nationen nach Kräften. Sie errichteten Flüchtlingslager und versuchten, Familien, die das Kriegsschicksal in alle Winde verstreut hatte, wieder zusammenzuführen. Es war eine langwierige und herzzerreißende Aufgabe.

A la fin de l'été 1945, des millions de gens désorientés et sans domicile étaient en fuite – à travers l'Europe et l'Extrême-Orient. Ils étaient à la recherche d'un endroit où vivre et, pour beaucoup d'entre eux, cela signifiait un nouveau pays.

C'était une époque de changements. Les vieilles puissances coloniales européennes avaient fait faillite. Des avenirs prometteurs avaient été fortement grevés d'hypothèques afin d'obtenir de l'argent pour la guerre. Et, pour s'assurer la coopération de leurs sujets, les anciens hommes politiques avaient fait des promesses qu'on leur demandait maintenant de tenir. L'Inde réclamait son indépendance. Les musulmans de ce sous-continent demandaient la partition. Les juifs voulaient une patrie qui leur appartienne. En Chine, aucune demande ne fut nécessaire. Les communistes se sont tout simplement arrogé ce qu'ils voulaient.

Dans tous ces endroits, on continuait à tuer. Durant sa première année, le nouvel Etat d'Israël dut affronter ses cinq voisins arabes. Mais, dans la réalité, le processus fut parfois d'une simplicité surprenante. Sans faire de bruit, la Grande-Bretagne rendit sa liberté à l'Inde.

Là où cela était possible, les Nations unies tout récemment créées faisaient ce qu'elles pouvaient pour aider, édifiant des camps pour les réfugiés, essayant de regrouper les familles qui avaient été séparées par les aléas de la guerre. Ce fut une tâche éprouvante et de longue haleine.

22 July 1946.
Ninety-one people
died when the King
David Hotel in
Jerusalem was blown
up by Zionists.

22. Juli 1946.
91 Menschen
starben, als Zioni-
sten das King David
Hotel in Jerusalem
in Schutt und Asche
legten.

22 juillet 1946.
Une bombe posée
par les sionistes tue
91 personnes à
l'Hôtel King David
de Jérusalem.

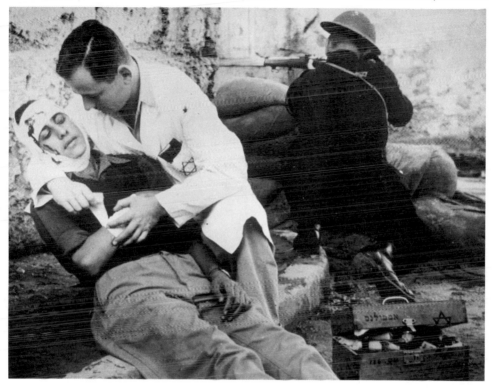

Bandages and bullets. A Jewish doctor tends a wounded man, while his comrade takes aim. The setting is the strife-ridden area of Palestine between Jewish Tel Aviv and the Arab city of Jaffa. The state of Israel was born in war, and spent its youth fighting for survival

Pflaster und Patronen. Ein jüdischer Arzt versorgt einen verwundeten Mann, während dessen Kamerad zum Schuß anlegt. Schauplatz ist der heiß umstrittene Streifen Palästinas, der zwischen dem jüdischen Tel Aviv und der arabischen Stadt Jaffa liegt. Der Staat Israel wurde im Krieg geboren und verbrachte seine Jugend damit, ums Überleben zu kämpfen.

Bandages et balles. Un médecin juif soigne un blessé tandis que son camarade ajuste sa cible. La scène se passe dans une zone de conflit de Palestine entre la Tel Aviv juive et la ville arabe de Jaffa. L'Etat d'Israël est né durant la guerre et il a passé sa jeunesse à se battre pour survivre.

An exodus that failed: British troops guard a trainload of Jews in Hamburg docks, 1947. The Jews on board had hoped to sail to Palestine in the first 'exodus' ship, *Ocean Vigour*. Instead, they were rounded up, to be sent to the Poppendorf Camp.

Ein Exodus, der fehlschlug: Britische Soldaten bewachen 1947 einen Zug mit Juden im Hamburger Hafen. Diese Juden hatten gehofft, auf dem ersten „Exodus"-Schiff, der *Ocean Vigour*, nach Palästina zu gelangen. Statt dessen wurden sie zusammengetrieben, um in das Lager Poppendorf befördert zu werden.

Un exode qui a échoué : des soldats britanniques gardent un train de juifs sur les quais de Hambourg, en 1947. Les juifs embarqués avaient espéré pouvoir rejoindre la Palestine par le premier bateau de l'« exodus », l'*Ocean Vigour*. Au lieu de cela, ils furent envoyés au camp de Poppendorf.

One of the ringleaders of the 'exodus' movement is placed
under arrest, to be taken under close guard to the camp
Coming so soon after the Holocaust, these traumatic echoes of
Auschwitz and Buchenwald inflamed Zionist feelings.

Ein Anführer der „Exodus"-Bewegung wird verhaftet und streng
bewacht ins Lager transportiert. Diese traumatischen Anklänge
an Auschwitz und Buchenwald erhitzten zionistische Gemüter.

L'un des fomentateurs de l'« exodus » est placé sous mandat
d'arrêt avant d'être interné au camp. Se produisant si tôt
après l'Holocauste, ces rappels traumatisants d'Auschwitz et
de Buchenwald ont enflammé les sentiments sionistes.

An exodus that succeeded: Jewish refugees struggle ashore from the SS *United States*, February 1948. The ship beached near Haifa, after evading British patrol boats on the voyage from Bari, Italy. On board were 700 Jews from Central Europe.

Ein Exodus, der gelang: Jüdische Flüchtlinge verlassen im Februar 1948 das Dampfschiff SS *United States* und kämpfen sich an Land. Das Schiff wurde in der Nähe von Haifa auf Sand gesetzt, nachdem es britische Patrouillenboote auf seiner Überfahrt von Bari in Italien erfolgreich umschifft hatte. An Bord befanden sich 700 Juden aus Mitteleuropa.

Un exode réussi : des réfugiés juifs rejoignent le rivage après avoir quitté le SS *United States*, en février 1948. Le navire parti de Bari, en Italie, s'était échoué près de Haïfa après avoir échappé aux bateaux de patrouille britanniques. Il avait à son bord 700 juifs originaires d'Europe centrale.

Jewish refugees on their way to Palestine, 1945, photographed by Erich Auerbach. On many of the refugee ships, the conditions were appalling – overcrowded, lacking food and water, no knowledge of how long the journey would take, and always the fear that the ship would be intercepted.

Jüdische Flüchtlinge auf dem Weg nach Palästina, 1945 von Erich Auerbach fotografiert. Auf vielen Flüchtlingsschiffen herrschten entsetzliche Zustände – Überfüllung, Nahrungs- und Wasser-mangel, Unkenntnis der Reisedauer und stets die Angst, daß das Schiff abgefangen werden könnte.

Réfugiés juifs en route vers la Palestine en 1945, photographiés par Erich Auerbach. Les conditions de voyage furent souvent dramatiques – embarcations bondées, ni eau ni nourriture, sans savoir combien de temps durerait la traversée et, toujours, la peur d'être intercepté.

British troops question a young Jewish refugee on her
arrival at Haifa in 1945. Within weeks of the end of
the war the exodus began.

Britische Soldaten befragen 1945 ein jüdisches
Flüchtlingsmädchen bei seiner Ankunft in Haifa. Bereits
wenige Wochen nach Kriegsende setzte der Exodus ein.

Soldats britanniques interrogeant une jeune réfugiée
juive à son arrivée à Haïfa en 1945. L'exode commença
quelques semaines après la fin de la guerre.

Calcutta, August 1946. Rioting flared between Hindus and Muslims when the British announced their plans to withdraw from the Indian subcontinent, and to create the separate states of India and Pakistan.

Kalkutta, August 1946. Zwischen Hindus und Moslems brachen Unruhen aus, als die Briten ankündigten, daß sie sich aus dem indischen Subkontinent zurückziehen und die getrennten Staaten Indien und Pakistan gründen würden.

Calcutta, août 1946. Des émeutes éclatent entre hindous et musulmans lorsque les Britanniques annoncent leur intention de se retirer du sous-continent indien et de créer deux Etats séparés, l'Inde et le Pakistan.

Calcutta police use tear gas to clear the streets. Over 2,000 people were killed in the riots, and 4,000 injured. At this stage it was feared that partition would lead inevitably to civil war.

Polizisten in Kalkutta setzen Tränengas ein, um die Straßen zu räumen. Über 2 000 Menschen verloren bei den Unruhen ihr Leben und 4.000 wurden verletzt. Zu diesem Zeitpunkt fürchtete man, daß eine Teilung unausweichlich zum Bürgerkrieg führen würde.

La police de Calcutta utilisa des gaz lacrymogènes pour repousser les manifestants. Plus de 2 000 personnes furent tuées au cours de ces émeutes, et 4 000 blessées. A ce moment-là, on craignit que la division n'entraînât inéluctablement la guerre civile.

July 1945. Indian leader Jawaharlal Nehru addresses a huge crowd from the balcony of his house in Simla. The movement for Indian independence had gained strength during the war, many Indians refusing to fight on the British side.

Juli 1945. Das indische Oberhaupt Jawaharlal Nehru spricht zu einer riesigen Menschenmenge vom Balkon seines Hauses in Simla. Die indische Unabhängig-keitsbewegung hatte während des Krieges zugenommen, denn viele Inder lehnten es ab, auf seiten der Briten zu kämpfen.

Juillet 1945. Le leader indien Jawaharlal Nehru s'adresse à une foule gigantesque depuis le balcon de sa maison, à Simla. Le mouvement pour l'indépendance de l'Inde s'est affermi durant la guerre, de nombreux Indiens refusant de se battre aux côtés des Britanniques.

2 February 1948. The body of Mohandas Gandhi lies in state at Birla House, New Delhi. His Hindu assassin opposed Gandhi's policy of communal and religious tolerance. 'The light has gone out of our lives and there is darkness everywhere,' mourned prime minister Nehru.

2. Februar 1948. Der aufgebahrte Leichnam Mahatma Gandhis im Birla House in Neu-Delhi. Der hinduistische Attentäter lehnte Gandhis Politik der gemeinschaftlichen und religiösen Toleranz ab. „Das Licht ist aus unserem Leben verschwunden, und uberall herrscht Dunkelheit", trauerte Ministerpräsident Nehru.

2 février 1948. La dépouille du Mahatma Gandhi est exposé à la Birla House, à New Delhi. Son assassin hindou était opposé à la politique de tolérance politique et religieuse de Gandhi. « La lumière s'est éteinte dans notre vie et l'obscurité a tout enveloppé », déclara le Premier ministre Nehru.

Bombay, 21 August 1947. When partition finally came, it was greeted with huge joy by Hindus and Muslims alike, though Gandhi himself took little part in the celebrations. He was in Calcutta, trying to calm both Hindus and Muslims.

Bombay, 21. August 1947. Als die Teilung schließlich kam, nahmen sie Hindus und Moslems mit großer Freude auf, obwohl Gandhi selbst an den Feierlich-keiten nicht teilnahm. Er befand sich nämlich in Kalkutta und versuchte, die dortigen Hindus und Moslems zu beschwichtigen.

Bombay, 21 août 1947. Lorsque la partition fut finalement proclamée, elle fut accueillie avec allégresse autant par les hindous que par les musulmans, bien que Gandhi lui-même ait peu participé aux cérémonies. Il se trouvait à Calcutta, essayant de calmer et les hindous et les musulmans.

Karachi, 22 August 1947.
Muslim crowds attend
Id prayers at the mosque.

Karatschi, 22. August 1947.
Große Menschenmengen von
Moslems nehmen an den
Id-Gebeten der Moschee teil.

Karachi, 22 août 1947. Une
immense foule de musulmans
se prosterne pour la prière à
la mosquée.

Last years of the Raj, 1945. Earl Wavell, Viceroy of India (in pith helmet) watches Indian children eating at the Rotary Club free kitchen in south Calcutta. Wavell was succeeded by Lord Louis Mountbatten in March 1947.

Die letzten Jahre der britischen Oberherrschaft in Indien, 1945. Graf Wavell, Vizekönig von Indien (mit Tropenhelm), mit indischen Kindern bei der Armenspeisung des Rotary Clubs in Süd-Kalkutta. Wavells Nachfolge trat im März 1947 Lord Louis Mountbatten an.

Les dernières années du Raj, en 1945. Le comte Wavell, vice-roi des Indes (en casque colonial) observe de petits Indiens mangeant à la cuisine en plein air du Rotary Club, dans le sud de Calcutta. Le successeur de Wavell fut Lord Louis Mountbatten, en mars 1947.

Last days of the Raj,
August 1947.
Viceroy Lord
Mountbatten and his
wife are surrounded
by children in
New Delhi, only
days before Indian
independence.

Die letzten Tage der
britischen Oberherr-
schaft in Indien,
August 1947. Eine
Schar von Kindern
umringt Vizekönig
Lord Mountbatten
und seine Ehefrau,
wenige Tage bevor
Indien die
Unabhängigkeit
erlangt.

Les derniers jours
du Raj, août 1947.
Le vice-roi Lord
Mountbatten et son
épouse entourés par
des enfants de New
Delhi, quelques jours
seulement avant
l'accession à
l'indépendance de
l'Inde.

Brave newcomers to an old world, 1948. Recently arrived Jamaican immigrants in London study a map of the Underground. Large numbers of West Indians arrived after the war in response to invitations from UK-based companies.

Mutige Neulinge in einer alten Welt, 1948. Immigranten aus Jamaika, die erst vor kurzem in London angekommen sind, studieren eine U-Bahn-Karte. Zahlreiche Westinder folgten nach dem Krieg der Einladung britischer Firmen.

De braves nouveaux venus dans un vieux monde, en 1948. Des immigrants jamaïcains récemment arrivés à Londres étudient un plan du métro. Un grand nombre d'habitants de Caraïbe débarquèrent après la guerre, attirés par des sociétés ayant leur siège au Royaume-Uni.

July 1949. A newly
arrived West Indian
immigrant looks
for lodgings in
Liverpool. They may
not be easy to find.

Juli 1949. Ein
soeben eingetroffener
westindischer Ein-
wanderer sieht sich
in Liverpool nach
einer Unterkunft um.
Die Suche wird nicht
einfach sein.

Juillet 1949.
Un émigrant arrivant
tout droit des
Caraïbes cherche un
logement à
Liverpool. Ce qui
n'était sans doute pas
chose facile.

Brave newcomers to a new world, 1940. Nobel laureate
Albert Einstein and his wife Margot take the oath of allegiance
to become citizens of the United States. Einstein's secretary,
Rene Dakas, is on the extreme left.

Mutige Neulinge in einer neuen Welt, 1940. Nobelpreisträger
Albert Einstein und seine Frau Margot schwören den
Fahneneid, um die Staatsbürgerschaft der Vereinigten Staaten zu
erwerben. Ganz links steht Einsteins Sekretärin, Rene Dakas.

De braves nouveaux venus dans un nouveau monde, en 1940.
Le lauréat du prix Nobel, Albert Einstein, et son épouse Margot
prêtent serment d'allégeance pour devenir citoyens des Etats-
Unis. A l'extrême-gauche, la secrétaire d'Einstein, Rene Dakas.

The slow lane, August 1940. Immigrants crowd Brooklyn Post Office to register for US citizenship. They have four months to complete the process. Each one will be fingerprinted and screened before admission to 'the greatest democracy in the world'.

Die Kriechspur, August 1940. Immigranten drängen sich im Postamt von Brooklyn, um die amerikanische Staatsbürgerschaft zu beantragen. Für den Abschluß des Vorgangs haben sie vier Monate Zeit. Von jedem Einwanderer werden Fingerabdrücke genommen und seine Person wird überprüft, bevor er in „die größte Demokratie der Welt" aufgenommen wird.

Longue file d'attente, août 1940. Le bureau de poste de Brooklyn est rempli d'immigrants demandant la nationalité américaine. Ils ont quatre mois pour suivre la procédure. Chacun d'eux doit remettre ses empreintes digitales et est interrogé avant d'être admis dans « la plus grande démocratie du monde ».

January 1946.
An UNRRA official
checks the
nationalities of
arrivals at a
displaced persons'
camp near Germany.

Januar 1946. Eine
Beamtin der UNRRA
überprüft die Staats-
angehörigkeit von
Neuankömmlingen
in einem Flüchtlings-
lager nahe der
Grenze zu Deutsch-
land.

Janvier 1946.
Une fonctionnaire de
l'UNRRA vérifie la
nationalité des
arrivants dans un
camp pour
personnes déplacées,
près de l'Allemagne.

January 1946.
Men of the Royal
Artillery check the
countries sending
delegates to the
first UN conference
in London.

Januar 1946.
Angehörige der
britischen Artillerie
überprüfen die
Länder, die eine
Delegation zur
ersten UN-Konfe-
renz nach London
schicken.

Janvier 1946.
Des hommes de
l'Artillerie royale
vérifient les pays
envoyant des
délégations à la
première conférence
de l'ONU à Londres.

# 7. Showbusiness
# Das Showgeschäft
# Le show-business

'Don't sit under the apple tree with anyone else
but me, till I come marching home...' The
close harmony serenading of the Andrews Sisters
was the epitome of the sound of the Forties.

„Sitz unter unserem Apfelbaum immer nur mit
mir, bis ich wiederkehr'...“ Die Ständchen
der Andrews Sisters im Barbershop-Stil waren
der Inbegriff des Sounds der vierziger Jahre.

« Ne passe aucune heure avec une autre sous
notre prommier, jusqu'au jour de mon retour... »
La sérénade mièvre des Andrews Sisters était la
chanson type des années Quarante.

# 7. Showbusiness
# Das Showgeschäft
# Le show-business

There were those who believed that Hollywood won the war. It wasn't just a matter of Errol Flynn capturing Burma single-handed, or Walter Pigeon rescuing the British Expeditionary Force from Dunkirk. Hollywood thrust its stars into selling war bonds, entertaining troops, running the stage door canteen, keeping alive the American Dream. Films ran off the production line like tanks or planes. The studio system was at its best and busiest.

Radio audiences numbered tens of millions. In Britain the aural gems included Tommy Handley's *ITMA*, *Workers' Playtime*, and the new *Desert Island Discs* series. In the United States there was *The Jack Benny Show*, *The Bing Crosby Show* and *Burns and Allen*. Of the non-professional broadcasters, only Churchill and the British Nazi propagandist 'Lord Haw-Haw' achieved comparable fame.

While the war lasted, dancers, actors, musicians and entertainers signed up for ENSA – officially 'Entertainments National Service Association', sarcastically 'Every Night Something Awful'. They performed in factories and improvised theatres, on the backs of lorries, in aircraft hangars, even on the decks of ships. The quality varied, the response was always enthusiastic.

And for those who performed in night clubs, there were still enough customers to keep the Scotch flowing, if not the champagne.

Eigentlich war Hollywood der große Gewinner des Krieges. Nicht nur, weil Errol Flynn im Alleingang Burma eingenommen oder Walter Pigeon das britische Expeditionskorps aus Dünkirchen gerettet hatte. Hollywoods Stars verkauften Kriegsanleihen, unterhielten die Soldaten, betreuten die Essensausgabe am Bühneneingang und hielten den Amerikanischen Traum am Leben. Filmproduktionen rollten ebenso vom Fließband wie Panzer oder Flugzeuge.

Am Radio saßen zig Millionen Menschen. In Großbritannien gehörten zu den beliebtesten

Sendungen Tommy Handley's *ITMA*, *Workers' Playtime* und die neue Serie *Desert Island Discs*. In den Vereinigten Staaten gab es *The Jack Benny Show*, *The Bing Crosby Show* sowie *Burns and Allen*. Lediglich Churchill und der britische Nazi-Propagandist „Lord Haw-Haw" erreichten unter den nicht professionellen Radiosprechern einen vergleichbaren Bekanntheitsgrad.

Solange der Krieg andauerte, verpflichteten sich Tänzer, Schauspieler, Musiker und Alleinunterhalter der ENSA – offiziell „Entertainments National Service Association", sarkastisch „Every Night Something Awful". Sie traten in Fabriken, auf improvisierten Theaterbühnen, auf Ladeflächen von LKWs, in Flugzeughallen und selbst auf Schiffsdecks auf. Die Qualität der Darbietungen war unterschiedlich, der Beifall stets stürmisch.

Und in den Nachtclubs gab es noch immer genügend Besucher, um den Scotch, wenn auch keinen Champagner, in Strömen fließen zu lassen.


Certains croyaient que Hollywood avait gagné la guerre. Il ne s'agissait pas seulement d'Errol Flynn conquérant la Birmanie en un tournemain, ni de Walter Pigeon sauvant le Corps expéditionnaire britannique de Dunkerque. Hollywood envoya ses vedettes vendre des emprunts de guerre, divertir les troupes, remplir les cantines à l'entrée des artistes, maintenir en vie le rêve américain. Les films étaient produits au même rythme que les chars ou les avions.

Les auditeurs de radio se comptaient en dizaines de millions. En Grande-Bretagne, les émissions les plus populaires étaient l'*ITMA* de Tommy Handley, *Worker's Playtime* et le nouveau feuilleton *Desert Island Discs*. Aux Etats-Unis, il y avait *The Jack Benny Show*, *The Bing Crosby Show* et *Burns and Allen*. Seuls Churchill et « Lord Haw-Haw », le propagandiste nazi britannique, réalisaient des scores comparables à ces professionnels de la radio.

Tandis que la guerre faisait encore rage, danseurs, acteurs, musiciens et comiques signaient pour l'ENSA – officiellement « Entertainments National Service Association », surnommée ironiquement « Every Night Something Awful ». Ils donnaient des représentations dans des usines et des théâtres improvisés, sur des plateaux de camions, dans des hangars à avions ou même sur des ponts de bateaux. Si la qualité était variable, l'accueil était toujours enthousiaste.

Et, pour ceux qui se produisaient dans les boîtes de nuit, il y avait toujours suffisamment de consommateurs pour faire couler le whisky à défaut de champagne.

Hollywood stars in the real world. Colonel James Stewart returns to America
on the troopship *Queen Elizabeth* after a tour of duty in Europe (above).
Captain Clark Gable at work with the guns of a Flying Fortress (right).

Hollywood-Stars in der wirklichen Welt. Oberst James Stewart kehrt von Europa
auf dem Truppentransportschiff *Queen Elizabeth* nach Amerika zurück (oben).
Hauptmann Clark Gable an den Geschützen einer Flying Fortress (rechts).

Des stars de Hollywood se plongent dans le monde réel. Le colonel James
Stewart rentre en Amérique sur le transporteur de troupes *Queen Elizabeth*
après une tournée du devoir en Europe (ci-dessus). Le capitaine Clark Gable
armant une mitrailleuse de Forteresse volante (à droite).

British and Hollywood film star David Niven in the role of compère
for a concert given by Glenn Miller and the Band of the AEF
in London, 1944. Niven was an army officer throughout the war.

Der Hollywood-Filmstar David Niven in der Rolle eines
Conférenciers bei einem Konzert Glenn Millers und des AEF-
Orchesters in London, 1944. Niven diente die gesamte Kriegszeit
über als Offizier.

David Niven, vedette de cinéma britannique et hollywoodienne,
dans un rôle de comparse lors d'un concert donné par Glenn Miller
et son orchestre à l'AEF, à Londres en 1944. Niven a été officier
de l'armée durant toute la guerre.

The most famous band of World War II: Glenn Miller at
work in a London club. Later that year, while flying to France,
Miller's plane disappeared. His death is still a mystery.

Das berühmteste Orchester des Zweiten Weltkrieges. Glenn
Miller in einem Londoner Club. Im gleichen Jahr verschwand
Millers Flugzeug auf dem Weg nach Frankreich. Sein Tod ist
bis heute ein Rätsel geblieben.

L'orchestre le plus célèbre de la Seconde Guerre mondiale :
Glenn Miller dans un club de Londres. L'avion de Glenn
Miller disparut un peu plus tard cette année-là lors d'un vol
vers la France. Sa mort n'a jamais été élucidée.

GIs cluster round Marlene Dietrich, 'somewhere in France', 1945. Dietrich
was born in Berlin, but left for Hollywood in 1930. Hitler ordered her back
to Germany, but she refused, and became an Allied idol during the war.

GIs umringen 1945 Marlene Dietrich „irgendwo in Frankreich". Die
gebürtige Berlinerin war 1930 nach Hollywood gegangen. Hitler beorderte
sie zwar nach Deutschland zurück, aber die Dietrich lehnte ab und wurde
während des Krieges zu einem Idol der Alliierten.

Des GI entourent Marlene Dietrich « quelque part en France » en 1945.
Née à Berlin, Marlene Dietrich a émigré à Hollywood en 1930. Hitler lui
ordonna de rentrer en Allemagne, mais elle refusa et devint l'idole des
Alliés pendant toute la guerre.

Hudson River, August 1945. Marlene Dietrich's million-dollar legs are seen hovering over the water on her return to the United States on the *Queen Elizabeth* after entertaining the troops in Europe.

Hudson River, August 1945. Marlene Dietrich kehrt nach einer Kriegstournee in Europa auf der *Queen Elizabeth* in die Vereinigten Staaten zurück. Ihre sensationell langen Beine schweben hier über dem Wasser des Flusses.

Hudson River, août 1945. Marlene Dietrich exhibe ses jambes légendaires au-dessus de l'eau lors de son retour aux États-Unis à bord du *Queen Elizabeth*, après avoir diverti les troupes américaines en Europe.

Dancers at the Windmill Theatre in London rehearse in gas masks and tin hats. Apart from a compulsory closure for two weeks in September 1939, the Windmill was the only London theatre that stayed open throughout the war. For years afterwards, it proudly boasted, 'We never closed.'

Tänzerinnen im Windmill-Theater in London proben in Gasmasken und Stahlhelmen. Abgesehen von einer Zwangsschließung für zwei Wochen im September 1939 war dies das einzige Theater Londons, das den ganzen Krieg über geöffnet blieb. Noch Jahre später rühmte es sich stolz: „Wir schlossen nie".

Des danseuses du Windmill Theatre, à Londres, répètent en masque à gaz et casque en fer blanc. Hormis une fermeture forcée de deux semaines en septembre 1939, le Windmill Theatre a été le seul théâtre de Londres resté ouvert durant toute la guerre. Pendant des années, il proclama ensuite fièrement « Nous n'avons jamais fermé ».

Kurt Hutton's
portrait of the British
singer, Vera Lynn.
She was dubbed 'The
Forces' Sweetheart'.

Kurt Huttons Porträt
der britischen Sänge-
rin Vera Lynn.
Man nannte sie „Der
Liebling der Armee".

Portrait de la
chanteuse
britannique Vera
Lynn par Kurt
Hutton. Elle était
surnommée « La
fiancée de l'armée ».

The young Francis
Albert Sinatra,
gangly crooner from
Hoboken, New
Jersey, and darling of
the bobbysoxers.

Der junge Francis
Albert Sinatra
aus Hoboken in
New Jersey, ein
schlaksiger Sänger
romantischer Lieder,
war der Liebling
der amerikanischen
Teenager.

Le jeune Francis
Albert Sinatra,
crooner efflanqué,
de Hoboken, New
Jersey, faisait fondre
le cœur des
adolescentes.

2 June 1945. A delighted Josephine Baker embarrasses a British lance-corporal
at a Victory party. Famous as a dancer and singer in the Thirties, Josephine Baker
spent most of the war as a volunteer in the Free French Women's Air Auxiliary.

2. Juni 1945. Josephine Baker ist sichtlich erfreut über die Verlegenheit eines
britischen Obergefreiten bei einer Siegesfeier. In den dreißiger Jahren eine
berühmte Tänzerin und Sängerin verbrachte Josephine Baker den größten Teil
des Krieges als Freiwillige in der Luftwaffenhilfstruppe der Freien Französinnen.

2 juin 1945. Une Josephine Baker prise de fou rire embarrasse un caporal
britannique lors d'une fête de la victoire. Célèbre danseuse et chanteuse des années
trente, Josephine Baker a consacré la plupart de son temps pendant la guerre
comme volontaire des femmes auxiliaires de l'armée de l'air de la France libre.

May 1947. Lucille
Ball sings in the rain
at a New York
charity torchlight
procession.

Mai 1947. Lucille
Ball singt im
Regen bei einem
wohltätigen Fackel-
zug in New York.

Mai 1947. Lucille
Ball chante sous la
pluie lors d'un défilé
de charité aux
flambeaux à New
York.

Another dirty rat
hits the canvas.
Screen tough guy
James Cagney
practises his judo
throws, July 1947.

Und wieder landet
eine dreckige Ratte
auf der Matte. James
Cagney, der knall-
harte Bursche der
Filmwelt, trainiert
im Juli 1947, wie
man seine Gegner zu
Boden wirft.

Un autre sale renégat
est projeté contre le
tatami. James
Cagney, le dur à
l'écran, fait une
démonstration de
prises de judo, en
juillet 1947.

'Here's another fine mess you've gotten me into…' Oliver Hardy in an unlikely role as a ballet star in the 1943 film *The Dancing Masters*.

„Da hast du mich ja wieder in einen schönen Schlamassel hineingezogen …" Oliver Hardy in einer ungewöhnlichen Rolle als Startänzer in dem Film *The Dancing Masters* aus dem Jahre 1943.

« Tu m'as encore fichu dans un drôle de pétrin… » Oliver Hardy dans un rôle inhabituel de petit rat de l'opéra pour le film *The Dancing Masters* tourné en 1943.

Stan Laurel plays a
ballerina in the same
film, which was not
a great success, but
the routines had a
charm all their own.

Stan Laurel spielt
eine Ballerina im
selben, nicht beson-
ders erfolgreichen
Film, dessen
Tanzeinlagen aber
dennoch einen ganz
eigenen Charme
besitzen.

Dans le même film,
Stan Laurel joue le
rôle d'une ballerine.
Ce ne fut pas un
grand succès, mais
les scènes de danse
valaient leur pesant
de rire.

Screen gangster becomes a football fan, November 1942. Like many Hollywood celebrities, Edward G Robinson (in profile, left) came to Europe to entertain Allied troops. The Studio bosses, most of them Jewish, encouraged their stars to do what they could in the struggle against Nazism.

Ein Leinwand-Gangster wird zum Fußballfan, November 1942. Wie viele andere Hollywood-Persönlichkeiten kam auch Edward G. Robinson (im Profil, links) nach Europa, um die Truppen der Alliierten zu unterhalten. Die amerikanischen Studiobosse, größtenteils Juden, ermutigten ihre Stars, den Kampf gegen den Nationalsozialismus nach Kräften zu unterstützen.

Un gangster du cinéma devient fan de football, en novembre 1942. Comme de nombreuses autres célébrités de Hollywood, Edward G. Robinson (de profil, à gauche) est venu en Europe pour divertir les troupes alliées. Les chefs de studio, juifs le plus souvent, encourageaient leurs vedettes à faire tout leur possible pour lutter contre le nazisme.

October 1948. Ingrid Bergman and Alfred Hitchcock, off duty during the filming of *Under Capricorn*. They visited Bow Street, the Tower of London and the George at Southwark. The film was described as 'a pretty fair disaster'.

Oktober 1948. Ingrid Bergman und Alfred Hitchcock in einer Pause während der Dreharbeiten zu *Under Capricorn*. Sie besuchten Bow Street, den Londoner Tower und das George (Gasthaus) in Southwark. Die Kritiker bezeichneten den Film allerdings als „eine ziemliche Katastrophe".

Octobre 1948. Ingrid Bergmann et Alfred Hitchcock, pendant une pause sur le tournage du film *Les Amants du Capricorne*. Ils visitèrent Bow Street, la Tour de Londres et le George à Southwark. Le film fut un véritable « bide »,

The biggest 'Hallo' in show business. Mickey Rooney arrives at Southampton on 1 January 1948 for an engagement at the London Palladium.

Das größte „Hallo" im Showgeschäft. Mickey Rooney trifft am 1. Januar 1948 in Southampton ein, um sein Engagement im Londoner Palladium anzutreten.

Le plus grand « Hallo » du show-business. Mickey Rooney à son arrivée à Southampton, le 1er janvier 1948, pour un engagement au London Palladium.

Sixteen-year-old
Elizabeth Taylor
joins the crowds to
watch the Lord
Mayor's Show,
1948. She had come
to London to film
*Conspirator*.

Die sechzehnjährige
Elizabeth Taylor
mischt sich 1948
unter die Schau-
lustigen, die sich die
Lord Mayor's Show
ansehen. Sie war
nach London
gekommen, um den
Film *Conspirator*
zu drehen.

Elizabeth Taylor,
alors âgée de 16 ans,
se joint à la foule
pour assister au Lord
Mayor's Show en
1948. Elle était
venue à Londres
pour le tournage du
film *Conspirator*.

Yves Montand, French singer and actor, signs autographs for his fans in the summer of 1949. It was a good year for Montand. He met Simone Signoret, and fell in love with her at first sight, and was invited to sing at the wedding of Rita Hayworth and Ali Khan.

Im Sommer 1949 schreibt der französische Sänger und Schauspieler Yves Montand Autogramme für seine Fans. Es war ein gutes Jahr für Montand: Er lernte Simone Signoret kennen, in die er sich auf den ersten Blick verliebte, und wurde gebeten, auf der Hochzeit von Rita Hayworth und Ali Khan zu singen.

Yves Montand, le chanteur et acteur français, signe des autographes pour ses fans durant l'été 1949. Ce fut une bonne année pour Montand, il rencontra Simone Signoret pour qui il eut le coup de foudre et fut invité à chanter au mariage de Rita Hayworth et d'Ali Khan.

Between marriages: Rita Hayworth signs up for her fans, 1948. It was the year that she
separated from her second husband Orson Welles, and the year in which she starred
with him in *The Lady from Shanghai*. The following year she married Prince Ali Khan.

Zwischen zwei Ehen: Rita Hayworth gibt 1948 Autogramme. In diesem Jahr trennte
sie sich von ihrem zweiten Ehemann, Orson Welles, und stand gleichzeitig mit ihm
für *Die Lady von Shanghai* vor der Kamera. Im darauffolgenden Jahr heiratete sie Prinz
Ali Khan.

Entre deux mariages : Rita Hayworth distribuant des dédicaces en 1948. Cette année-
là, elle se sépara de son second mari, Orson Welles, et, toujours cette année-là,
elle tourna avec lui *La Dame de Shanghai*. L'année suivante, elle épousait le prince
Ali Khan.

# 8. Design for living
# Alltagsdesign
# Art de vivre

The man who re-drew the fashion books: French
couturier Christian Dior poses with two of his models
in 1949. Two years earlier he had introduced the 'New
Look', featuring narrow shoulders and long, full skirts.

Der Mann, der die Mode-Handbücher neu zeichnete:
Im Jahr 1949 posiert der französische Couturier
Christian Dior mit zwei Mannequins. Zwei Jahre zuvor
hatte er den „New Look" eingeführt, den eine schmale
Schulterlinie und lange, üppige Röcke charakterisieren.

L'homme qui redessina les catalogues de mode :
le couturier français Christian Dior posant avec deux
de ses mannequins en 1949. Deux ans plus tôt, il avait
présenté le New Look, avec haut près du corps et
longue jupe évasée.

# 8. Design for living
## Alltagsdesign
## Art de vivre

The United States invasion of Europe had begun before the war. American design, culture and style had trickled across the Atlantic, bringing with it milk bars, streamlining, and cinemas built like Moorish palaces.

In the Forties the trickle became a flood. Hollywood led the way, for Hollywood was always at the forefront of fashion. The stars wore clothes and costumes that were as far removed from 'Austerity' and 'Utility' as chewing gum was from a carrot.

Until 1945, 'glamour' for Europeans meant 'uniform', but khaki serge has a limited appeal. For those that could afford it, one of the joys of peace was to return to out-and-out luxury. Christian Dior led the way with his 'New Look'. Architects once more put their dreams on paper, but capital was scarce in Europe and few dreams came true. In old-fashioned factories, swords were turned into ploughshares of pre-war design.

Science and technology leapt forward during the Forties. By the end of the decade, nations had at their disposal rocket propulsion, atomic power, the jet engine, radar, the earliest forms of artificial intelligence and the ballpoint pen. In some cases they didn't know what to do with their new toys. In others, sadly, they did.

Bereits vor dem Zweiten Weltkrieg hatte die Invasion Europas von seiten der Vereinigten Staaten begonnen. Der „American Way of Life" hinterließ überall seine Spuren, in den Milchbars, im stromlinienförmigen Design und in den maurischen Palästen nachempfundenen Kinos.

In den vierziger Jahren wurde der amerikanische Einfluß noch stärker. Das schon immer stilbildende Hollywood übernahm die Führung in der Mode. Seine Stars trugen Kleider und Kostüme, die sich nicht gerade durch „Einfachheit" und „Zweckmäßigkeit" auszeichneten.

„Glamour" bedeutete für Europäer bis 1945 „Uniform", aber die khakifarbene Serge besaß nur eine sehr begrenzte Anziehungskraft. Für die besser Gestellten brachte der Frieden die Rückkehr zu vollkommenem Luxus. Christian Dior bestimmte die Mode mit seinem „New Look", Architekten setzten ihre Ideen auf Papier um. Allerdings wurden nur wenige Entwürfe realisiert, denn in Europa mangelte es an Kapital. In altmodischen Fabriken schmiedete man Schwerter zu Pflugscharen im Design der Vorkriegszeit.

In Wissenschaft und Technologie gelangen in den Vierzigern wichtige Entwicklungen und Entdeckungen. Am Ende des Jahrzehnts gehörten der Raketenantrieb, die Atomkraft, das Düsentriebwerk, der Radar, die frühesten Formen künstlicher Intelligenz und der Kugelschreiber zum täglichen Leben. In manchen Fällen wußten die Nationen ihre neuen Spielzeuge nicht so recht zu nutzen, in anderen leider schon.

L'invasion de l'Europe par les Etats-Unis avait commencé avant la Seconde Guerre mondiale. Le design, la culture et le style américains avaient franchi l'Atlantique, amenant avec eux milkbars, profilages et cinémas ressemblant à des palais des mille et une nuits.

Dans les années quarante, le petit filet se transforma en fleuve. Hollywood montra la voie, car Hollywood a toujours été à la pointe de la mode. Les vedettes portaient des vêtements et des costumes aussi éloignés de l'«austérité» et de l'«utilité» que le chewing-gum peut l'être de la carotte.

Jusqu'en 1945, pour les Européens, «glamour» signifiait «uniforme», mais la serge kaki n'a qu'un attrait limité. Pour ceux qui pouvaient se le permettre, l'une des joies de la paix fut le retour du luxe sans restrictions. Christian Dior montra la voie avec son New Look. Une fois de plus, les architectes couchèrent leurs rêves sur le papier, mais il régnait une pénurie de capitaux en Europe et bien peu de ces rêves devinrent réalité. Dans les usines vétustes, les épées étaient transformées en charrues dans le style de l'avant-guerre.

La science et la technologie progressèrent durant les années quarante. A la fin de la décennie, l'humanité connaissait la fusée, l'énergie nucléaire, les moteurs à réaction, les radars, des formes primitives d'intelligence artificielle et le stylo bille. Parfois, on ne savait que faire de ces nouveaux jouets. Dans d'autres cas, hélas, on ne le savait que trop bien.

War time 'Utility', 1942. Clothes were rationed on a 'points' system which assigned a value to articles and permitted customers to 'spend' a certain number of total points, taking into account the type and amount of material used.

„Zweckmäßigkeit" zu Kriegszeiten, 1942. Kleidung war nach einem „Punkte"-system rationiert. Der Wert eines Artikels setzte sich auch aus Art und Menge des verwendeten Materials zusammen. Den Kunden stand nur eine bestimmte Gesamtsumme an Punkten für ihren „Kauf" zu Verfügung.

« Utilité » de temps de guerre, en 1942. Les vêtements étaient rationnés selon un système de « points » qui attribuait une certaine valeur aux articles et permettait aux acheteurs de « dépenser » un certain nombre de leur total de points prenant en compte la nature et la quantité du matériau utilisé.

An elegant lady
wearing Dior's 'New
Look' gets a critical
appraisal from a
passer-by on the
streets of London,
1949.

Eine elegante Dame,
die den „New Look"
trägt, erntet 1949 in
den Straßen Londons
den kritischen
Seitenblick einer
Passantin.

Une rue de Londres
en 1949. Une
passante observe
d'un œil critique une
élégante portant une
création New Look
de Dior.

Calculating both price and 'points'. A woman examines stockings after the
introduction of clothes rationing. Clothes coupons (tickets entitling the holder to a
ration), as well as food and petrol coupons, fed a busy and profitable black market.

Die Berechnung des Preises und der „Punkte". Eine Frau begutachtet Strümpfe nach
der Einführung der Bekleidungsrationierung. Bekleidungsgutscheine (Karten, die
den Besitzer zu einer Ration berechtigten) sowie Lebensmittel- und Benzingutscheine
hielten einen geschäftigen und gewinnbringenden Schwarzmarkt am Leben.

Calculer à la fois prix et « points ». Une femme examine des bas après l'introduction
du système de rationnement des vêtements. Les tickets de rationnement, qu'il s'agisse
de vêtements (tickets autorisant le titulaire à obtenir une ration) ou de nourriture et
de carburant, alimentaient un marché noir animé et profitable.

July 1941. A solution to the problem of clothes rationing. Women in a Croydon store have their legs painted to resemble stockings. The 'points' thus saved could be used for other clothes.

Juli 1941. Eine Lösung des Problems der Bekleidungsrationierung. Frauen lassen sich in einem Geschäft in Croydon „Strümpfe" aufmalen. Die auf diese Art gesparten „Punkte" konnten für andere Kleidungsstücke verwendet werden

Juillet 1941. Une solution au problème du rationnement des vêtements. Des femmes dans un magasin de Croydon se font peindre les jambes pour faire croire qu'elles portent des bas. Les « points » ainsi économisés pouvaient être utilisés pour d'autres vêtements.

A British fashion show, March 1949. The show was primarily for overseas buyers. Desperate to boost exports, Britain was making a bold attempt to enter the international fashion market.

Eine britische Modenschau im März 1949, die sich in erster Linie an Kunden aus Übersee richtete. Da der Exporthandel dringend angekurbelt werden mußte, wagte Großbritannien einen kühnen Versuch, in den internationalen Modemarkt vorzustoßen.

Un défilé de mode britannique en mars 1949. Il était destiné en premier lieu aux acheteurs d'outremer. Souhaitant ardemment relancer ses exportations, la Grande-Bretagne faisait tout pour conquérir le marché international de la mode.

November 1941.
Anne Scott James,
of the *Picture Post*
magazine, poses
for an article entitled
'Should Women
Wear Trousers?'
When this picture
was taken, hundreds
of thousands
already were.

November 1941.
Anne Scott James
von der Zeitschrift
*Picture Post* posiert
für einen Artikel mit
dem Titel „Sollten
Frauen Hosen
tragen?" Als diese
Aufnahme entstand,
taten dies bereits
Hunderttausende
von Frauen.

Novembre 1941.
Anne Scott James,
de la revue *Picture
Post*, pose pour un
article intitulé « Les
femmes devraient-
elles porter des
pantalons ? » Quand
cette photo fut prise,
des centaines de
femmes le faisaient
déjà.

July 1948. It was a glorious summer, and a wonderful time to be showing off new 'swimwear', although in those days you called them 'bathing costumes'. The bottle of wine, camera and binocular case indicate that this is one of Bill Brandt's posed fashion shots.

Juli 1948. Es war ein herrlicher Sommer und eine wunderbare Zeit, um diese neue Bademode vorzuführen, die man immer noch „Badeanzug" nannte. Weinflasche, Kamera und Fernglasetui deuten darauf hin, daß diese Modeaufnahme von Bill Brandt stammt.

Juillet 1948. Ce fut un été magnifique et une époque merveilleuse pour s'exhiber dans ces nouveaux maillots de bain qu'on appelait encore « costumes de bain ». La bouteille de vin, l'appareil photo et l'étui à jumelles indiquent qu'il s'agit là d'une photo de mode de Bill Brandt, qui n'avait rien improvisé.

July 1946.
A Casino de Paris
dancer models
the sensational
new 'bikini' at the
Molitor Pool in
Paris.

Juli 1946. Eine
Tänzerin des Casino
de Paris führt den
sensationellen neuen
„Bikini" am Molitor
Pool in Paris vor

Juillet 1946. Une
danseuse du casino
de Paris présente
le sensationnel
nouveau « bikini »,
à la piscine Molitor
de Paris.

Opera returns to
Glyndebourne.
Composer Benjamin
Britten (seated)
and singer Peter
Pears discuss a score.

Die Oper kehrt nach
Glyndebourne
zurück. Komponist
Benjamin Britten
(sitzend) und Sänger
Peter Pears bespre-
chen eine Partitur.

Retour de l'opéra
à Glynbourne.
Le compositeur
Benjamin Britten
(assis) et le chanteur
Peter Pears discutant
une scène.

A nest of left-wing poets, 1949. From left to right: W H Auden,
Cecil Day Lewis and Stephen Spender at a literary conference in
Italy. Auden had spent the war years in the United States.

Ein Treffen politisch linksstehender Dichter, 1949. Von links
nach rechts: W. H. Auden, Cecil Day Lewis und Stephen
Spender bei einer Literaturkonferenz in Italien. Auden hatte
die Kriegsjahre in den Vereinigten Staaten verbracht.

Trois écrivains gauchisants, en 1949. De gauche à droite :
W. H. Auden, Cecil Day Lewis et Stephen Spender lors d'un
congrès de littérature en Italie. Auden a passé les années de
guerre aux Etats-Unis.

January 1945. Children queue in Harrods for the autograph of
celebrated children's writer Enid Blyton. Her Noddy character was
still a few years away, but the Famous Five were well established.

Januar 1945. Kinder stehen im Kaufhaus Harrods Schlange für
ein Autogramm der gefeierten Kinderbuchautorin Enid Blyton.
Ihre „Noddy"-Figur entstand zwar erst einige Jahre später, aber
die „Fünf Freunde" waren bereits wohl etabliert.

Janvier 1945. Des enfants font la queue chez Harrods pour
obtenir une dédicace d'Enid Blyton, célèbre écrivain pour enfants.
Son personnage de Noddy était déjà âgé de quelques années,
mais le Club des cinq était très populaire.

Novelist and critic Pamela Hansford Johnson (left) talking with novelist Olivia Manning (right) at the opening of the British PEN (Poets, Essayists, Novelists) Club headquarters in Chelsea, February 1949.

Die Schriftstellerin und Kritikerin Pamela Hansford Johnson (links) im Gespräch mit der Schriftstellerin Olivia Manning (rechts) anläßlich der Eröffnung des britischen PEN-Clubs (Poets, Essayists, Novelists) in Chelsea im Februar 1949.

La romancière et critique Pamela Hansford Johnson (à gauche) s'entretenant avec sa collègue Olivia Manning à l'inauguration du quartier général du Club PEN (Poets, Essayists, Novelists), à Chelsea, en février 1949.

Picasso in exile,
Paris 1948. The
artist had sworn not
to return to his
native Spain while
Franco ruled there.

Picasso im Pariser
Exil, 1948. Der
Künstler hatte
geschworen, nicht in
sein Geburtsland
Spanien zurückzu-
kehren, solange
Franco dort regierte.

Picasso en exil
à Paris en 1948.
L'artiste avait juré
de ne pas retourner
dans son Espagne
natale tant que
Franco la
gouvernerait.

Henry Moore, 1948. After working as an official war artist, Moore returned to his studies of semi-abstract female forms and family groups in the late 1940s.

Henry Moore, 1948. Nachdem er als offizieller Kriegskünstler gearbeitet hatte, kehrte Moore in den späten vierziger Jahren zu seinen halbabstrakten Frauenformen und Familiengruppen zurück.

Henry Moore, en 1948. Après avoir travaillé comme artiste de guerre officiel, Moore retourna à ses études de formes féminines semi-abstraites et de groupes familiaux vers la fin des années quarante.

Michael Redgrave chairs a meeting of Equity, the actors' trade union, in 1946. Some members are still in battledress. As with most other workers, the war years had provided full employment for the acting profession.

Michael Redgrave im Vorsitz einer Versammlung von Equity, der Gewerkschaft der Schauspieler, im Jahre 1946. Einige Mitglieder tragen noch immer Uniformen. Die Kriegsjahre hatten bei den Schauspielern, ebenso wie bei den meisten Arbeitern, für Vollbeschäftigung gesorgt.

Michael Redgrave présidant une séance de l'Equity, le syndicat des acteurs, en 1946. Certains membres sont encore en treillis. Pour les acteurs comme pour beaucoup d'ouvriers, les années de guerre ont été synonymes de plein emploi.

Abram Games with the poster he designed to attract
recruits to the ATS. The women's army had previously
been seen as less glamorous than the navy or air force.

Abram Games vor seinem Plakat, das Rekruten für
den ATS (Auxiliary Territorial Service) anwerben
sollte. Diese Frauenarmee hatte vorher ein weniger
glanzvolles Image als die Marine oder die Luftwaffe.

Abram Games avec son affiche dessinée pour favoriser
l'engagement auprès de l'ATS. L'armee de temmes
avait auparavant moins de prestige que la marine ou
l'armée de l'air.

A multiple exposure photograph of prima ballerina
Margot Fonteyn, 1949. As in the other arts, ballet
reached a far wider audience during the war, and its
appeal increased throughout the 1940s.

Eine mehrfach belichtete Aufnahme der Primaballe-
rina Margot Fonteyn, 1949. Wie auch die anderen
schönen Künste erreichte das Ballett während
des Krieges ein viel breiteres Publikum, und seine
Anziehungskraft nahm im Laufe der vierziger Jahre
stetig zu.

Photographies superposées de la Prima ballerina
Margot Fonteyn, en 1949. Comme les autres arts,
le ballet a touché un public plus large durant la
guerre et sa popularité n'a cessé de croître pendant
les années quarante.

Forties triumphalism: the interior of an aeroplane hangar at Ortobello in Tuscany, designed by Italian architect and engineer Pier Luigi Nervi, 1940. Nervi used a latticework of reinforced concrete to create 'strength through form'.

Triumph der Vierziger: Der italienische Architekt und Ingenieur Pier Luigi Nervi entwarf 1940 diese Flugzeughalle in Ortobello in der Toskana. Nervi verwandte ein Gitterwerk aus Stahlbeton, um „Kraft durch Form" zu erzielen.

Le triomphalisme des années quarante : intérieur d'un hangar à avions à Ortobello, en Toscane, œuvre de l'architecte et ingénieur italien Pier Luigi Nervi, en 1940. Nervi a utilisé un treillis de béton armé pour générer « la sévérité par la forme ».

A soundproof room for acoustical research at the Bell Telephone Laboratories, Murray Hill, New Jersey. The walls, floor and ceiling are lined with fibreglass.

Ein schalldichter Raum für akustische Experimente in den Bell Telephone Laboratories in Murray Hill, New Jersey. Wände, Boden und Decke sind mit Fiberglas verkleidet.

Laboratoire insonorisé pour les recherches acoustiques chez Bell Telephone Laboratories, Murray Hill, New York, dans le New Jersey. Murs, sol et plafond sont recouverts de fibre de verre.

Arctic Test. A 1948 Morris Oxford is put through
the freeze test. It had been left in 40 degrees of
frost for five days. The report proudly announced
that it started at 'the second time of asking'.

Arktischer Test. Ein 1948er Morris Oxford wird
dem Kältetest unterzogen. Man hatte ihn fünf
Tage lang einer Kälte von minus 40 Grad
ausgesetzt. Der Ergebnisbericht verkündete stolz,
daß er beim zweiten Versuch ansprang.

Test polaire. Une Morris Oxford de 1948 a été
exposée pendant cinq jours à une température
de moins 40 degrés. Le rapport déclare fièrement
qu'elle a démarré dès la seconde tentative.

Lightning Test. Three million volts hit a car at the Westinghouse Electric Corporation, Pittsburgh. The passenger, happily, was unharmed.

Blitztest. Drei Millionen Volt trafen ein Auto auf dem Gelände der Westinghouse Electric GmbH in Pittsburgh. Der Fahrer blieb zum Glück unverletzt.

Test de conductivité. Un éclair de trois millions de volts atteint une voiture à la Westinghouse Electric Corporation, à Pittsburgh. Dieu soit loué, le passager en est sorti indemne.

# 9. Sport and leisure
## Sport und Freizeit
## Sports et loisirs

March 1943. Stanley Matthews takes a corner for the RAF.
Matthews was labelled 'the best footballer the war has produced',
but his greatest moment was to come in 1953, when he created
three goals in 13 minutes in the FA Cup Final.

März 1943. Stanley Matthews führt für die Royal Air Force einen
Eckstoß aus. Matthews galt als „der beste Fußballer, den der
Krieg hervorgebracht hat". Den größten Erfolg seiner Laufbahn
verbuchte er aber 1953, als er im Endspiel um den Pokal der
Football Association innerhalb von 13 Minuten drei Tore schoß.

Mars 1943. Stanley Matthews tire un corner pour la RAF. Matthews
a été sacré « meilleur footballeur que la guerre ait engendré »,
mais son heure devait vraiment sonner en 1953, lorsqu'il marqua
trois buts en 13 minutes en finale de la Coupe de la FA.

# 9. Sport and leisure
## Sport und Freizeit
## Sports et loisirs

Even before the end of the war there were tasters of the sporting joys that lay ahead. Unofficial international matches were held, and crowds thronged to this less lethal rivalry. It hardly mattered what the sport was. Greyhound racing, speedway, TT (Tourist Trophy) motorcycle races, ice hockey, even the Oxford and Cambridge Boat Race attracted tens of thousands.

By 1946 sport had returned to normal. England's cricketers were thrashed by Australia, and their tennis players crashed out of the singles at Wimbledon. Liverpool were top of the Football League. The World Series had resumed in the States. Americans had won the four major golf tournaments. Joe Louis had emphasized his right to be World Heavyweight champion.

Grounds were packed. Fans had waited a long time to see their favourite teams in action again. Even the bottom clubs in the English Football League could guarantee gates of 15,000 week after week. Tragedy struck when over 65,000 people crammed into Burnden Park, Bolton, to see the game against Stoke. A barrier collapsed. Thirty-three people were killed.

The first post-war Olympic Games were held in London in 1948. The United States topped the table of medal winners, Sweden was second, France third. At the end of the Games a number of athletes from Eastern European countries defected to the West.

Selbst während des Krieges konnte man Kostproben der zukünftigen sportlichen Freuden genießen: Zu den inoffiziellen internationalen Spielen strömten die Zuschauer in Scharen herbei, um diese unblutigen Rivalitäten mitzuerleben. Um welche Sportart es sich handelte, spielte keine große Rolle. Windhund-, Speedway- oder Motorradrennen, der Tourist Trophy, Eishockey oder sogar die Regatta zwischen Oxford und Cambridge zogen Zehntausende an.

Bis 1946 hatte sich der Sport wieder normalisiert. Englands Kricketmannschaft wurde von Australien geschlagen, die australischen Tennisspieler schieden in Wimbledon im Einzel aus,

Liverpool stand an der Spitze der Fußballiga, in den Vereinigten Staaten hatte die World Series im Baseball wieder begonnen, die Amerikaner gewannen die vier wichtigsten Golfturniere und Joe Louis behauptete seinen Weltmeistertitel im Schwergewicht.

Die Stadien waren gut gefüllt, denn die Fans hatten lange darauf gewartet, ihre Lieblingsteams wieder live zu erleben. Sogar die Schlußlichter der englischen Fußballiga konnten Woche für Woche Zuschauerzahlen von 15.000 Besuchern verbuchen. Ein tragischer Unfall ereignete sich, als sich über 65.000 Zuschauer in das Stadion von Burnden Park in Bolton zwängten, um das Spiel gegen Stoke zu sehen. Eine Absperrung brach, und 33 Menschen kamen ums Leben.

Die ersten Olympischen Spiele nach Kriegsende fanden 1948 in London statt. Die Vereinigten Staaten führten die Liste der Medaillengewinner an, gefolgt von Schweden und Frankreich. Am Ende der Olympiade setzten sich zahlreiche osteuropäische Athleten in den Westen ab.

Avant même la fin de la guerre, on eut un avant-goût des joies sportives à venir. On organisa des rencontres internationales, mais inofficielles, et les foules se pressaient, poussées par une rivalité moins meurtrière. La nature de la discipline sportive ne jouait pas un grand rôle. Courses de lévriers, épreuves de vitesse, grand prix de moto du Tourist Trophy, hockey sur glace, et même la régate d'aviron entre Oxford et Cambridge attiraient des milliers de spectateurs.

En 1946, le sport était revenu à la normale. Les joueurs de cricket d'Angleterre furent étrillés par l'Australie et ceux de tennis, éliminés des simples à Wimbledon. Liverpool était le club roi de la Football League. Les World Series avaient repris aux Etats-Unis, les Américains remportant quatre des plus grands tournois de golf. Joe Louis avait souligné la légitimité de son titre de champion des poids lourds.

Les gradins étaient combles. Les fans avaient attendu longtemps pour revoir leurs équipes favorites. Même les clubs de bas de tableau de la première division de football anglaise pouvaient garantir dans les 15 000 entrées semaine après semaine. Une tragédie éclata lorsque plus de 65 000 personnes s'agglutinèrent dans Burnden Park, à Bolton, pour assister au match contre Stoke. Une barrière s'effondra. 33 personnes furent tuées.

Londres fut le théâtre des premiers Jeux olympiques de l'après-guerre en 1948. Les Etats-Unis décrochèrent le plus grand nombre de médailles, devant la Suède et la France. A la fin des Jeux olympiques, un certain nombre d'athlètes de pays d'Europe de l'Est passèrent à l'Ouest.

November 1945. Ken Joy takes a 'bidon' of milk and
sugar during his successful bid to break the London to
Brighton cycle speed record.

November 1945. Ken Joy stärkt sich mit einer Flasche
gesüßter Milch während seines erfolgreichen Versuchs,
den Fahrrad-Geschwindigkeitsrekord auf der Strecke von
London nach Brighton zu brechen.

Novembre 1945. Ken Joy s'empare d'un « bidon » de lait
et de sucre durant sa tentative, réussie, de battre le
record de vitesse à vélo sur la distance Londres-Brighton.

December 1949.
Von Bueren's cycle
disintegrates as he
wins the Swiss
Championships in
Zurich. Siegenthaler
finishes second, but
intact.

Dezember 1949.
Bei den Schweizer
Meisterschaften in
Zürich bricht von
Buerens Rennrad
gerade in dem
Moment aus-
einander, als er siegt.
Siegenthaler wird
Zweiter, sein Rad
bleibt aber intakt.

Décembre 1949.
La bicyclette de von
Bueren se casse au
moment même où il
remporte le
championnat suisse à
Zurich. Siegenthaler
termine deuxième,
mais son vélo reste
intact.

A contentious issue in the 1990s: a *fait accompli* in the 1940s. The referee
raises Miss Italy's hand in triumph after she knocks out Miss England in
an unlikely-looking international tournament in Stockholm, 1949.

Ein umstrittenes Thema in den neunziger Jahren: eine vollendete Tatsache
in den Vierzigern. Der Schiedsrichter hebt die Faust der siegreichen
Miß Italien, nachdem sie Miß England in einem kurios anmutenden
internationalen Turnier in Stockholm 1949 k. o. geschlagen hat.

Question de contentieux en 1990 : un fait accompli dans les années
quarante. L'arbitre brandit, en signe de triomphe, la main de Miss Italie
qui a mis K.-O. Miss Angleterre, lors d'un tournoi international à
Stockholm en 1949.

December 1947. World Heavyweight champion Joe Louis pins Jersey Joe Walcott against the ropes at Madison Square Garden, New York. Louis won on points. A year later he KO-ed Walcott. Two years later, Louis retired.

Dezember 1947. Der Weltmeister im Schwergewicht, Joe Louis, bedrängt Jersey Joe Walcott im Madison Square Garden in New York. Louis gewann nach Punkten. Ein Jahr darauf schlug er Walcott k. o. Zwei Jahre später setzte er sich zur Ruhe.

Décembre 1947. Le champion du monde des poids lourds, Joe Louis, catapulte Jersey Joe Walcott dans les cordes au Madison Square Garden de New York. Louis gagna aux points. Un an plus tard, il mettra Walcott K.-O., avant de raccrocher ses gants de boxe deux ans plus tard.

Frank Swift,
England's goalkeeper
in the 1940s. He
was among those
killed in the Munich
air crash of 1958.

Frank Swift, Englands
Torhüter der vierziger
Jahre. Er gehörte
zu den Passagieren,
die 1958 bei einem
Flugzeugabsturz in
München ums Leben
kamen.

Frank Swift, gardien
de but international
de l'Angleterre dans
les années quarante.
Il était dans l'avion
qui s'écrasa à Munich
en 1958.

Emil Zatopek of
Czechoslovakia,
September 1947.
A year later he was
the surprise winner
of the 10,000 metres
at the London
Olympic Games.

Emil Zátopek aus
der Tschechoslowa-
kei im September
1947. Ein Jahr
später war er der
Überraschungssieger
über 10.000 Meter
bei den Olympischen
Spielen in London.

Le Tchèque Emil
Zátopek, septembre
1947. Un an plus
tard, à la surprise
générale, il gagnera
le 10 000 mètres aux
Jeux olympiques de
Londres.

American servicemen brought jitterbugging to Britain during the war. It became a craze. A couple step out at the Paramount Salon de Danse, Tottenham Court Road, London (above), while young beboppers hit the timber at the Club Eleven (right).

Amerikanische Militärangehörige initiierten in Großbritannien die Jitterbug-Mode. Diesen Jazztanz zeigt ein Paar im Paramount Salon de Danse in Londons Tottenham Court Road (oben), während junge Anhänger des Bebop im Club Eleven ebenfalls eine flotte Sohle aufs Parkett legen (rechts).

Ce sont des militaires américains qui, durant la guerre, lancèrent le jitterbug en Grande-Bretagne, où il fit des ravages. Couple plein d'élan au Paramount Salon de Danse, Tottenham Court Road, à Londres (ci-dessus), tandis que de jeunes danseurs de be-bop brûlaient les planches au Club Eleven (à droite).

Jitterbugging in
London, 1949.
To the old it was
depraved, to the
young it was joyous.

Der Jitterbug in
London, 1949.
Für die Alten
versinnbildlichte er
Verdorbenheit, für
die Jungen bedeutete
er Spaß.

Jitterbug à Londres
en 1949. Ce qui
semblait dépravé aux
anciens était une
source de plaisir
pour les jeunes.

Jitterbugging in
Paris, 1949.
The only difference
would appear to
be the footwear.

Der Jitterbug in
Paris, 1949. Der
einzige Unterschied
besteht scheinbar
nur im Schuhwerk.

Jitterbug à Paris
en 1949. La seule
différence porte
sur le choix des
chaussures.

Victory Leap. Young tennis players at an Essex junior championship, August 1945. Sadly, ten years were to pass before an English player was to win a Grand Slam championship. Angela Mortimer won the French Open in 1955.

Siegessprung. Junge Tennisspieler bei einer Meisterschaft der Junioren in Essex im August 1945. Leider mußte England noch zehn Jahre warten, bis es endlich einen Grand-Slam-Titel errang: Angela Mortimer gewann 1955 die French Open.

Le bond de la victoire. Jeunes joueurs de tennis lors d'un championnat junior dans l'Essex en août 1945. Malheureusement, il fallut attendre dix ans avant qu'un joueur britannique remporte un match du Grand Slam. Angela Mortimer gagna l'Open de France en 1955.

The Playing Fields of
Eton, November
1947. Collegers and
Oppidans enjoy
the mudbath of the
Wall Game.

Der Sportplatz von
Eton im November
1947. Privatschüler
wie staatliche
Schüler haben Spaß
an der gemeinsamen
Schlammschlacht
beim Mauerballspiel.

Terrain de jeux à
Eton, novembre
1947. Des élèves
d'écoles privées et
publiques apprécient
le bain de boue du
jeu de balle au mur.

A holidaymaker scans the horizon for signs of the Cowes Regatta, August 1949. The sweater is the height of Forties fashion.

Ein Urlauber sucht im August 1949 den Horizont nach Booten der Regatta von Cowes ab. Sein Pullunder entspricht der Mode der vierziger Jahre.

Vacancier scrutant l'horizon lors des régates de Cowes, en 1949. Son débardeur est à la pointe de la mode dans les années quarante.

The British seaside
two months after
D-day, August 1944.
Bournemouth begins
to return to normal.

Die britischen See-
bäder zwei Monate
nach dem Tag X,
August 1944. In
Bournemouth findet
man zum normalen
Alltag zurück.

Plage britannique
deux mois après le
Jour J, en août
1944. Bournemouth
revient lentement à
une vie normale.

The Games That Never Were. Japanese women display a banner decorated with pearls valued at £6,000. The Games were cancelled.

Die Spiele, die nie stattfanden. Japanerinnen führen eine Flagge vor, die Perlen im Wert von etwa 6.000 Pfund schmücken. Die Olympischen Spiele in Japan wurden abgesagt.

Les jeux qui n'eurent jamais lieu. Des Japonaises déploient un drapeau décoré de perles d'une valeur de 6 000 livres. Les Jeux olympiques furent annulés.

The last of a relay of runners brings the torch from Athens into the stadium at London for the start of the 1948 Olympic Games.

Der Schlußläufer einer Staffel tragt die Fackel aus Athen in das Londoner Stadion, so daß die Olympischen Spiele von 1948 eröffnet werden können.

Le dernier des relayeurs amène la torche olympique en provenance d'Athènes au stade de Londres pour l'inauguration des Jeux olympiques de 1948.

# 10. Children
# Kinder
# Les enfants

February 1940, east coast of England. The weapons of war were often treated as playground accessories by children, sometimes with disastrous results. For this boy, it would seem the worst that could happen would be to drop his ice cream.

Februar 1940, an der Ostküste Englands. Kinder nutzten Kriegswaffen häufig wie Turngeräte auf einem Spielplatz, was mitunter katastrophale Folgen hatte. Das Allerschlimmste für diesen Jungen wäre wohl, seine Eiswaffel fallen zu lassen.

Février 1940, côte Est de l'Angleterre. Pour les enfants, les armes de guerre étaient souvent comme les accessoires d'un terrain de jeu, qui eut parfois des conséquences dramatiques. Quant à ce petit garçon, le pire qui semble pouvoir lui arriver est de laisser tomber son cornet de glace.

# 10. Children
# Kinder
# Les enfants

Babies like routine: children prefer a life that's spiced with the unexpected. And the early 1940s were full of the unexpected. For British boys and girls, there were disruptions at any time of the day or night: troops marching through town, air raids, bomb sites to explore, scrap metal to be collected for the 'war effort'. Schools were suddenly moved hundreds of miles to a safer location. Popular and unpopular teachers left to do their bit. Mums and dads were busy 20 hours out of the 24.

Pocket money was almost non-existent, but then, there was little enough to buy anyway. Toy factories were all turned over to war production, and after the war everything, it seemed, was 'for export' only. 'Make do and mend' applied every bit as much to playthings as to evening dresses or motor cars.

But what a time to fantasize! You could be Monty or Rommel in the desert, or an air ace in the Battle of Britain, or a film star like Betty Grable, or a heroine of the Resistance. You could march to glory, fight your way across whole continents, be a glamorous spy, save your comrades, even if it made you late for dinner.

But for many thousands of other children, reality was not fun, but death and disaster.

Babys lieben noch feste Gewohnheiten; Kinder hingegen bevorzugen ein Leben voller Überraschungen – so wie es die frühen vierziger Jahre boten. Zu jeder Tages- und Nachtzeit ereigneten sich interessante Zwischenfälle und es gab Neues zu entdecken: Soldaten, die durch die Stadt marschierten, Fliegeralarm, Trümmergrundstücke, die erforscht werden wollten, und Altmetall, das im Rahmen der „Kriegsanstrengungen" gesammelt wurde. Schulen wurden um Hunderte von Kilometern in ein sichereres Gebiet verlegt, die Lehrer zogen an die Front. Mütter und Väter waren 20 Stunden am Tag beschäftigt.

Taschengeld gab es so gut wie keins, aber schließlich konnte man auch kaum etwas kaufen. Die Spielzeugfabriken waren der Kriegsproduktion unterstellt worden, und nach Kriegsende schien alles nur „für den Export" bestimmt zu sein. „Begnüge dich mit dem, was du hast, und repariere es", galt ebenso für Spielsachen wie für Abendkleider oder Autos.

Aber was für eine Zeit zum Träumen! Man konnte Montgomery oder Rommel in der Wüste sein. Man konnte ein Fliegeras in der Schlacht um England, ein Filmstar wie Betty Grable oder eine Heldin der Widerstandsbewegung sein. Man konnte dem Ruhm entgegenmarschieren, sich seinen Weg durch ganze Kontinente kämpfen, ein schillernder Spion sein oder seine Kameraden retten, selbst wenn man darüber zu spät zum Essen kam.

Für Tausende anderer Kinder war das wirkliche Leben jedoch kein Spaß, sondern bedeutete nur Tod und Unglück.


Les bébés aiment la routine ; les enfants préfèrent une vie riche en surprises. Et le début des années quarante n'en manquait vraiment pas. Pour les petits garçons et petites filles britanniques, il y avait des distractions à tout instant du jour et de la nuit : des troupes défilant en ville, des raids aériens, des zones bombardées à explorer, de la ferraille à récupérer pour les « efforts de guerre ». Les écoles furent transférées à des centaines de kilomètres dans des lieux plus sûrs. Les professeurs étaient partis au front. Les parents étaient occupés vingt heures par jour.

L'argent de poche était le plus souvent inexistant et, quand on en avait, on ne savait pas quoi acheter. Les usines de jouets s'étaient adaptées à la production de guerre et, après la guerre, sembla-t-il, tout était destiné « aux exportations » exclusivement. « Faites faire et réparer », était la devise aussi bien pour les jouets que les robes du soir ou les voitures.

Mais quelle époque pour laisser courir son imagination ! Vous pouviez être Monty ou Rommel dans le désert, un pilote de chasse invincible durant la bataille d'Angleterre, une star de cinéma comme Betty Grable, ou encore une héroïne de la résistance. Vous pouviez marcher vers la gloire, vous battre à travers des continents entiers, vous glisser dans la peau d'un espion, sauver vos camarades même si cela vous faisait arriver en retard pour le souper.

Cependant, pour des milliers d'autres enfants, la réalité ne fut pas plaisir, mais signifiait de mort et de catastrophe.

1940. Evacuee children take a last look at families and London before leaving for the countryside. One and a half million children were evacuated. Some enjoyed their new world, but many felt the strain of living with strangers in a land at war.

1940. Kinder, die evakuiert werden, werfen einen letzten Blick auf ihre Familien und auf London, bevor die Fahrt aufs Land beginnt. Eineinhalb Millionen Kinder wurden verschickt. Manche von ihnen freuten sich über die neue Umgebung, aber viele spürten die Belastungen eines Lebens unter fremden Menschen in einem Land, das Krieg führte.

1940. Des enfants disent au revoir à leurs familles et à Londres avant de partir pour la campagne. Un million et demi d'enfants furent ainsi évacués. Certains apprécièrent leur nouveau cadre de vie, mais beaucoup n'arrivèrent pas à s'habituer à vivre chez des étrangers dans un pays en guerre.

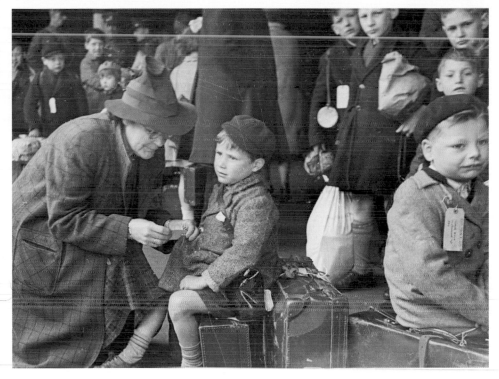

A happier journey: a volunteer helper fastens an identification label onto a child's coat at Paddington Station, May 1942. The children in this picture by Bert Hardy were going on holiday, not being evacuated.

Eine glücklichere Reise; Im Mai 1942 befestigt eine freiwillige Helferin einen Erkennungsanhänger am Mantel eines Kindes im Bahnhof Paddington. Die Kinder in dieser Aufnahme von Bert Hardy fuhren in die Ferien, nicht in die Evakuierung.

Un voyage plus heureux : une auxiliaire volontaire fixe un badge d'identification au manteau d'un enfant à la gare de Paddington, en mai 1942. Les enfants pris ici en photo par Bert Hardy partaient en vacances; ils n'étaient pas évacués.

July 1940. A ten-year-old girl, recently evacuated from the Channel port of Folkestone, helps out on a farm at Llanvetherine, near Abergavenny, Wales. There were many stories of the disbelief with which town children greeted the wonders of nature.

Juli 1940. Ein zehnjähriges Mädchen, das kurz zuvor aus der Kanalhafenstadt Folkestone evakuiert worden ist, hilft auf einem Bauernhof in Llanvetherine, in der Nähe von Abergavenny in Wales. Es kursierten viele Geschichten über das ungläubige Staunen, mit dem Stadtkinder den Wundern der Natur begegneten.

Juillet 1940 . Une petite fille de 10 ans récemment évacuée du port de Folkestone, sur la Manche, aide dans une ferme à Llanvetherine, près d'Abergavenny, au Pays de Galles. D'innombrables histoires relatent l'incrédulité des enfants des villes devant les merveilles de la nature.

Refreshment for
the thirsty. A young
evacuee takes a
glass of milk during
her journey.

Eine Erfrischung
für die Durstigen.
Auf ihrer Reise in
die Evakuierung
trinkt ein Mädchen
ein Glas Milch.

Remède contre
la soif. Une jeune
évacuée boit un
verre de lait durant
son voyage.

Schoolchildren form orderly files to march away from their concrete shelters after a practice alarm at Southgate, London, at the height of the Blitz. Shelters came in many shapes, sizes and materials.

Schulkinder verlassen in geordneten Reihen zur Zeit der schlimmsten deutschen Luftangriffe ihre Betonbunker nach einem Probealarm in Southgate, London. Bunker entstanden in zahlreichen Formen, Größen und Materialien.

Des écoliers se mettent sagement en rang pour quitter leurs abris en béton après une simulation d'alerte à Southgate, à Londres, au plus fort du Blitz. Il existait des abris de toute forme, taille et matériaux.

The original caption to this photograph reads: 'A family gives the thumbs up to a warden who warned them of a delayed action bomb he found in the vicinity of south east London.' In reality, the primitive shelter would have been of little help.

Die ursprüngliche Bildunterschrift zu dieser Aufnahme lautet: „Eine Familie bedeutet einem Schutzwart durch ein Zeichen mit dem Daumen, daß alles in Ordnung sei. Er hatte sie vor einer Bombe mit Zeitzünder gewarnt, die er in der Umgebung Südwest-Londons gefunden hatte." Wäre die Bombe explodiert, hätte der primitive Unterschlupf wohl kaum Schutz geboten.

La légende originale de cette photo déclare : « Une famille lève le pouce à l'intention d'un chef d'îlot qui l'a mise en garde. Il avait découvert une bombe intacte dans le voisinage, au sud-est de Londres. » En cas d'explosion, leur abri primitif n'aurait pas été d'un grand secours.

Newly created playground, 1946. Children play on a bomb site in the East End of London, just after the war. For many years the rubble and disorder of such areas fed the imagination of children.

Ein neuer Spielplatz, 1946. Kinder spielen kurz nach Kriegsende auf einem Trümmergrundstück in Ost-London. Noch viele Jahre lang nährten die Überreste und das Chaos solcher Gegenden die Fantasie der Kinder.

Un tout nouveau terrain de jeu, en 1946. Enfants jouant dans un quartier bombardé de l'East End de Londres, juste après la guerre. Durant des années, les gravats et le désordre de tels endroits alimentèrent l'imagination des enfants.

Newly destroyed
home, 1941.
An orphan in
Belarus, former
Soviet Union, cries
outside his shattered
family home.

Ein gerade zerstörtes
Heim, 1941.
Ein Waisenkind in
Belarus in der
ehemaligen
Sowjetunion weint
vor dem zer-
trümmerten Heim
seiner Familie.

Foyer tout juste
détruit, en 1941.
Un orphelin de
Biélorussie, ex-
Union soviétique,
en pleurs devant sa
maison ravagée.

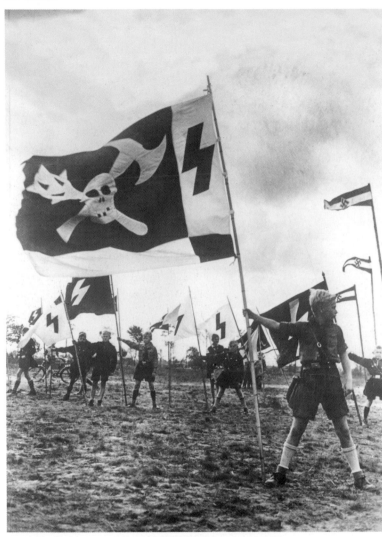

Young members of a
Nazi Youth group
proudly display their
flags at an open-air
camp near Berlin,
1940.

Im Jahre 1940
stellen Mitglieder
einer Jugendorgani-
sation der Nazis in
einem Zeltlager in
der Nähe von Berlin
stolz ihre Fahnen
zur Schau.

De jeunes membres
d'une unité des
Jeunesses hitlériennes
brandissent fièrement
leur drapeau dans
un camp de plein air
près de Berlin, en
1940.

Children gather behind a barbed wire fence at Auschwitz in the last few days of the war.

In den allerletzten Kriegstagen versammeln sich Kinder hinter einem Stacheldrahtzaun in Auschwitz.

Enfants agglutinés derrière une clôture en fil de fer barbelé à Auschwitz, durant les derniers jours de la guerre.

A Yugoslavian child
gives a hesitant Nazi
salute to a German
soldier, 1941.
The Yugoslav Royal
Army surrendered
on 17 April.

Ein jugoslawisches
Kind deutet 1941
einem deutschen
Soldaten gegenüber
zögernd den
Hitlergruß an.
Die Königliche
Armee Jugoslawiens
kapitulierte am 17.
April.

Un petit Yougoslave
fait un salut nazi
hésitant devant un
soldat allemand, en
1941. L'armée royale
de Yougoslavie s'est
rendue le 17 avril.

Thanksgiving Day, London, 26 November 1942. A US sergeant distributes candy to an ever-growing crowd of East End children. It wasn't long before every American serviceman was greeted with the phrase 'Got any gum, chum'.

Erntedankfest in London am 26. November 1942. Ein amerikanischer Feldwebel verteilt Süßigkeiten an eine immer größer werdende Schar Ost-Londoner Kinder. Bald wurde jeder amerikanische Militärangehörige mit dem Satz empfangen: „Haste'nen Kaugummi, Kamerad?"

Thanksgiving Day, Londres, 26 novembre 1942. Un sergent américain distribue des confiseries à une meute toujours plus grande d'enfants de l'East End. Il ne fallut pas attendre longtemps pour que chaque GI américain soit accueilli avec la ritournelle « Donne-nous des chewing-gums, mon homme ».

The thrills of the Saturday morning matinée. Children queue
for tickets at the Gaumont State Cinema, Kilburn, 1946.

Der besondere Reiz der Samstagmorgen-Vorstellung. Kinder
stehen 1946 am Gaumont State Cinema in Kilburn nach
Kinokarten an.

Les frissons de la séance de cinéma du samedi matin. Les
enfants font la queue pour acheter leur billet au Gaumont
State Cinema, à Kilburn, en 1946.

An infra-red photograph of a Saturday matinée. Even in the 1940s there was concern about the diet of fantasy and gun-toting drama.

Eine Infrarotaufnahme einer Samstagmorgen-Vorstellung. Schon in den vierziger Jahren war man über den Konsum von Fantasy- und Gewaltfilmen besorgt.

Photo aux infrarouges d'une séance de cinéma du samedi. Même dans les années quarante, on veillait à ne pas montrer de scènes de violence aux enfants.

The spoils of war, September 1940. Children in a south London street sort through fragments of shrapnel. Offically, such finds would be collected as part of the national war effort, but many found their way into private collections.

Kriegsbeute, September 1940. Kinder sortieren Schrapnell-Splitter in einer Straße in Süd-London. Offiziell wurden solche Funde im Rahmen der nationalen Kriegsanstrengungen eingesammelt. Viele Splitter gelangten jedoch in private Sammlungen.

Butin de guerre, septembre 1940. Dans une rue du sud de Londres, des enfants ramassent des éclats d'obus. Officiellement, ce genre de ramassage était censé faire partie de l'effort de guerre national, mais de nombreuses trouvailles devinrent des collections privées.

Lunchtime at a Düsseldorf school, 1946. The city was to become the richest in Germany, but that lay generations ahead.

Mittagessen in einer Düsseldorfer Schule, 1946. Generationen später sollte diese Stadt eine der wohlhabendsten in ganz Deutschland werden.

Heure de la cantine dans une école de Düsseldorf en 1946. La ville deviendra la plus riche d'Allemagne, mais seulement quelques décennies plus tard.

Hungarian boys outside their school, April 1945. The war in Europe is about to end. Hope has yet to come.

Ungarische Jungen vor ihrer Schule im April 1945. Der Krieg in Europa steht zwar kurz vor seinem Ende, die Hoffnung muß jedoch erst noch Fuß fassen.

Gamins hongrois devant leur école en avril 1945. La guerre est en passe de se terminer en Europe. L'espoir va resurgir.

January 1940. London children line up for a regulation spoonful of medicine from their teacher, Mr Jones. The children had been evacuated with their teacher and his wife to Heyshott in Sussex.

Januar 1940. Londoner Kinder stellen sich für den täglichen Löffel Medizin an, den ihnen ihr Lehrer, Mr. Jones, verabreicht. Die Kinder waren mit ihrem Lehrer und dessen Frau nach Heyshott in Sussex evakuiert worden.

Janvier 1940. De petits Londoniens font la queue pour se faire administrer une cuillerée de médicament par leur professeur, Mister Jones. Les enfants avaient été évacués avec leur professeur et sa femme à Heyshott, dans le Sussex.

December 1943. An apprehensive young girl receives her immunization injection against diphtheria. Plans were already being made for the brave new world that would be created once the war was over.

Dezember 1943. Ein ängstliches kleines Mädchen wird gegen Diphtherie geimpft. Es wurden bereits Pläne für die schöne, neue Welt nach dem Krieg geschmiedet.

Décembre 1943. Une fillette apeurée est vaccinée contre la diphtérie. On forgeait déjà des plans pour le monde meilleur qui serait créé une fois la guerre terminée.

# 11. All human life
## Menschliches, Allzumenschliches
## Les petits et les grands événements de la vie

'There was an old man with a beard, who said, It is just as I feared! Two owls and a hen, four larks and a wren have all built their nests in my beard.' A disciple of Edward Lear faces the rigours of 1940.

„Ich traf einen Alten mit Bart, der sagte: Das Leben ist hart! Zwei Eulen, ein Huhn, vier Lerchen – was nun? – bauten alle ihr Nest in den Bart." Ein Schüler Edward Lears blickt den Unbilden von 1940 tapfer ins Auge.

« Il y avait un vieil homme barbu qui déclarait : C'est exactement ce que j'avais craint ! Deux chouettes et un coq, quatre alouettes et un roitelet ont tous fait leur nid dans ma barbe. » Un disciple d'Edward Lear fait face aux rigueurs de 1940.

# 11. All human life
## Menschliches, Allzumenschliches
## Les petits et les grands événements de la vie

You didn't have to go far to find weirdness during the 1940s. Much of it was born of the war. People found themselves in situations that were unusual, unbearable, unfathomable. Such situations brought out the eccentric in the species.

It was a great age for trying to turn aside horror with humour. People wore funny clothes and gadgets. They put silly labels on their homes, their vegetables, their animals. They adapted the debris of war to novel and bizarre uses.

A lot of it was unintentional. If there was an air raid and a gas alert, you had to put on your tin helmet and your gas mask. With no petrol available, you felt compelled to turn your bicycle into a coal lorry, a delivery van, a taxi. Much of the humour, however, was deliberate. And there was often a photographer casting about for a picture that would bring a smile to the face of editor and reader.

If all else failed, you could find a man who could bend iron bars with his teeth, or lift incredible weights, or had a novel use for his hat, his beard, his trouser turn-ups. Women seemed not to bother with this sort of thing.

In den vierziger Jahren mußte man nicht lange suchen, um Seltsames zu finden. Viele Merkwürdigkeiten hatten ihren Ursprung im Krieg. Die ungewöhnliche, unergründliche und oft unerträgliche Situation brachte unweigerlich einige Exzentriker zum Vorschein.

Die Schrecken und das Greuel versuchte man durch Humor abzuwenden. Die Menschen trugen eigenartige Kleidung und Geräte. Sie befestigten alberne Schilder an ihren Häusern, ihrem Gemüse und ihren Tieren. Sie fanden neue und bizarre Verwendungszwecke für Kriegstrümmer.

Ein Teil der Heiterkeit war unfreiwilliger Natur. Gab es Fliegeralarm und eine Gaswarnung, mußte man sich mit Stahlhelm und Gasmaske verkleiden. Da kein Benzin zu haben war, mußte man notgedrungen sein Fahrrad in einen Kohlentransporter, einen Lieferwagen oder ein Taxi verwandeln. Ein großer Teil des Humors war allerdings sehr wohl beabsichtigt. Oft begegnete man einem Fotografen auf der Suche nach einem Bild, das dem Herausgeber wie dem Leser ein Lächeln aufs Gesicht zaubern würde.

Wenn alle Stricke rissen, konnte man einen Mann finden, der Eisenstangen mit den Zähnen verbog, unglaubliche Gewichte stemmte oder eine neue Verwendung für seinen Hut, seinen Bart oder die Aufschläge seiner Hosen gefunden hatte. Frauen schienen sich mit diesen Dingen keine Umstände zu machen.

L'étrangeté n'est jamais très loin pendant les années quarante. Souvent, elle a été engendrée par la guerre. Des gens se sont retrouvés dans des situations insolites, insupportables, insondables. Des situations qui mettent en exergue l'excentricité de l'espèce humaine.

Ce fut l'époque rêvée pour faire oublier l'horreur en faisant preuve d'humour. Certains arboraient des vêtements amusants et des gadgets. Ils donnaient des noms stupides à leurs maisons, leurs légumes, leurs animaux. Ils adaptaient les décombres de la guerre à des utilisations nouvelles et bizarres.

Beaucoup se faisait inconsciemment. En cas de raid aérien et d'alerte au gaz, vous étiez censés porter votre casque en fer blanc et votre masque à gaz. En l'absence d'essence, vous étiez bien obligé de transformer votre vélo en camion à charbon, camionnette de livraison, taxi. Bien de manifestations d'humour étaient toutefois délibérées. Et souvent un photographe était prêt à immortaliser une scène qui ferait sourire les éditeurs et leurs lecteurs.

Si rien d'autre ne marchait , vous pouviez trouver un homme capable de plier des barres de fer avec ses dents ou de soulever un poids incroyable ou qui avait une nouvelle utilisation pour son chapeau, sa barbe, ses bretelles. Les femmes ne semblaient pas se tracasser avec ce genre de choses.

Blindfold training for fire crews in Germany. The German firemen
are being trained to follow the sound of a gong. Three seem certain to
pass the test; one looks set to fail.

Ausbildung mit verbundenen Augen für Feuerwehrmannschaften in
Deutschland. Die deutschen Feuerwehrmänner üben, dem Klang
metallener Hammerschläge zu folgen. Drei von ihnen werden den Test
aller Wahrscheinlichkeit nach bestehen, einer wird wohl durchfallen.

Hommes masqués s'entraînant pour des équipes de pompiers en
Allemagne. Des pompiers allemands s'entraînent à se diriger vers le
son d'un gong. Trois semblent certains de réussir le test, l'autre n'est
vraiment pas dans la bonne voie.

Blindfold training for fire crews in Britain. The British firemen
are practising feeling their way in total darkness while wearing
respirators.

Ausbildung mit verbundenen Augen für Feuerwehrmannschaften
in Großbritannien. Die britischen Feuerwehrleute versuchen,
ihren Weg in völliger Dunkelheit zu ertasten, während sie
zusätzlich Atemschutzmasken tragen.

Hommes masqués s'entraînant pour des équipes de pompiers
en Grande-Bretagne. Des pompiers britanniques s'exercent
à savoir se diriger dans une obscurité totale tout en portant des
appareils respiratoires.

Gallant British War Effort, One: Sixty-year-old Home Guard Sergeant Gander balances a 130lb (60 kilo) bar on his head.

Tapfere britische Kriegsanstrengung Nr. 1: Der sechzig-jährige Feldwebel Gander, ein Mitglied der Bürgerwehr, balanciert ein Gewicht von 60 Kilogramm auf dem Kopf.

Vaillant effort de guerre britannique, scène un : le sergent Gander, âgé de 66 ans, membre des Territoriaux, avec, en équilibre sur la tête, une haltère de 60 kilos.

Gallant British War Effort, Two: Home Guardsman Joe Price,
a blacksmith by trade, bends an iron bar with his teeth.

Tapfere britische Kriegsanstrengung Nr. 2: Joe Price,
ebenfalls Mitglied der Bürgerwehr und von Beruf Schmied,
verbiegt eine Eisenstange mit den Zähnen.

Vaillant effort de guerre britannique, scène deux : Joe Price,
des Territoriaux et forgeron de son état, plie une tige d'acier
entre ses dents.

Life in a gas mask.
A Gloucester
policeman on traffic
duty, March 1941.

Leben mit der
Gasmaske.
Ein Verkehrspolizist
aus Gloucester
im Dienst im März
1941.

Vivre avec un
masque à gaz.
Un agent de police
de Gloucester
réglant la circulation
en mars 1941.

A member of the Auxiliary Fire Service takes a break from the Blitz, Christmas 1940. To many, there was something comic about the gas mask, and the many things you couldn't do while wearing one.

Ein Mitglied der Hilfstruppe der Feuerwehr amüsiert sich Weihnachten 1940 nach den deutschen Luftangriffen. Die Gasmaske entbehrte nicht einer gewissen Komik – besonders wegen der zahlreichen Dinge, die man nicht tun konnte, während man sie trug.

Un pompier auxiliaire fait une pause durant le Blitz, à Noël 1940. Le masque à gaz ne manquait pas d'un certain comique, ainsi que certaines choses que vous étiez incapables de faire si vous en portiez un.

December 1940.
A woman takes her
Christmas turkeys
home from
Maidstone market.
People were less
squeamish about
doing their own
slaughtering in the
1940s.

Dezember 1940.
Eine Frau fährt in
Maidstone ihre auf
dem Markt
gekauften
Weihnachtstruthähne
heim. Die Menschen
waren in den
vierziger Jahren, was
das Schlachten
anbetraf, weniger
empfindlich als
heute.

Décembre 1940.
Une femme
transporte ses dindes
pour Noël achetées
au marché de
Maidstone. Dans les
années quarante, les
gens étaient moins
scrupuleux quand il
s'agissait de tuer soi-
même des animaux.

Not as innocent
as it appears. These
salmon had been
poached from a local
stream in September
1943.

Nicht so unschuldig,
wie es scheint. Diese
Lachse wurden im
September 1943
in einem nahegelege-
nen Fluß illegal
gefangen.

Pas aussi innocent
qu'il y paraît : ces
saumons ont été
pêchés illégalement
dans une rivière des
environs en
septembre 1943.

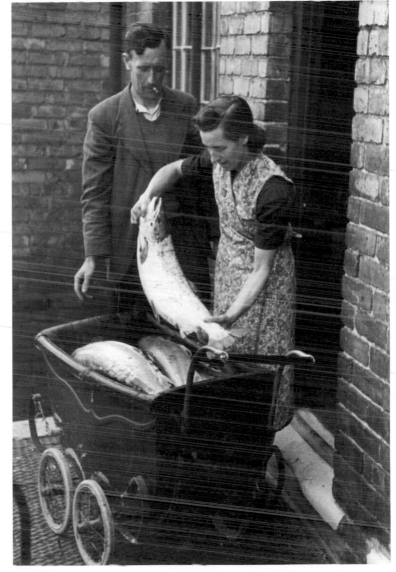

Georgie Porky. His Majesty King George VI
and one of his prize pigs regard each other
on the royal farm at Windsor, August 1942.
The King survived the war· the pig didn't.

Georgie Porky. Im August 1942 betrachten
Seine Majestät König Georg VI. und eines
seiner prämierten Schweine einander auf
dem königlichen Bauernhof in Windsor. Der
König überlebte den Krieg, das Schwein
nicht.

Georgie le porc. Tête à tête entre sa Majesté
le roi George VI et l'un de ses porcins primés,
à la ferme royale de Windsor, en août 1942.
Le roi a survécu à la guerre : ce ne fut pas le
cas du cochon.

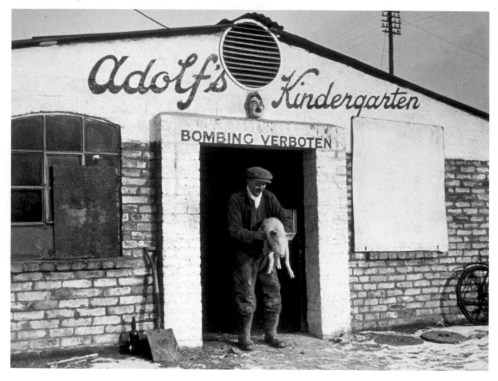

A dustman from Tottenham, London, holds one of his pigs (above). Pig-raising was strongly encouraged during the war. The little pig (right) was allegedly christened Hitler by its owner after it had tried to grab all the food from the rest of the litter.

Ein Angestellter der Müllabfuhr von Tottenham in London trägt eines seiner Schweine (oben). Die Schweinezucht wurde zu Kriegszeiten stark unterstützt. Das kleine Schwein (rechts) wurde angeblich von seinem Besitzer auf den Namen Hitler getauft, nachdem es versucht hatte, dem übrigen Wurf das gesamte Futter wegzuschnappen.

Un éboueur de Tottenham, à Londres, tient dans les bras l'un de ses cochons (ci-dessus). Elever des cochons était chaudement recommandé durant la guerre. Le porcelet de droite fut baptisé Hitler par son propriétaire, car il avait essayé de cacher toute sa nourriture sous le reste de la litière.

Fantasy football.
A pet parrot helps its
owner fill in a
wartime football
pool coupon.

Fantasie-Fußball-
ergebnis. Ein zahmer
Papagei hilft seinem
Besitzer während des
Krieges beim
Ausfüllen eines
Totoscheins.

Imagination d'un
joueur de loto.
Un perroquet
apprivoisé aide son
maître à remplir un
bulletin de loto
durant la guerre.

Waiting for the
'All Clear'. A bush
baby shelters in a tea
mug, March 1941.

Warten auf die
„Entwarnung". Ein
Buschbaby sucht im
März 1941 Schutz in
einem Teebecher.

En attendant que
le danger s'éloigne
Un galago s'abrite
dans une tasse à thé,
mars 1941.

The Long and the
Short of it: the
world's tallest man,
Ian van Albert,
nine feet (3 metres)
tall, poses beside
George Aslett, who
measures three feet
(1 metre).

Langer Rede kurzer
Sinn: Der größte
Mann der Welt, Ian
van Albert, der drei
Meter mißt, posiert
hier neben dem nur
einen Meter großen
George Aslett.

Le géant et le nain :
le plus grand homme
du monde, Ian van
Albert, toise du haut
de ses trois mètres
son adversaire
George Aslett qui lui
ne mesure qu'un
mètre.

January 1940.
A team of midgets
from the Earl's
Court Circus give
a helping hand to
the goalkeeper
at Fulham football
ground.

Januar 1940.
Ein Team von
Kleinwüchsigen,
Mitglieder des
Zirkus von Earl's
Court, unterstützt
den Torhüter auf
dem Fußballplatz
von Fulham.

Janvier 1940.
Une équipe de
benjamins de l'Earl's
Court Circus donne
un coup de main
au gardien de but au
stade de football
de Fulham.

Life in an 'iron lung'. A 16-month-old child at the Western Fever Hospital, London, July 1947 (above).
The child's condition was improving and he was able to breathe normally for six hours a day.
Kenneth Evans (right), a paralysed engineer, uses a microfilm device to enable him to read books.

Leben in der „Eisernen Lunge". Ein 16 Monate altes Kind (oben) im Western Fever Hospital in
London, Juli 1947. Der Gesundheitszustand des Kindes besserte sich, so daß es in der Lage war, sechs
Stunden am Tag normal zu atmen. Kenneth Evans (rechts), ein gelähmter Ingenieur, kann mit Hilfe
eines Mikrofilmgeräts Bücher lesen.

La vie dans un « poumon d'acier ». Un enfant âgé de 16 mois au Western Fever Hospital, Londres,
juillet 1947 (ci-dessus). L'état de l'enfant allait en s'améliorant et il put respirer normalement pendant
six heures par jour. Kenneth Evans (à droite), un ingénieur paralysé, utilise un système de microfilms
qui lui permet de lire.

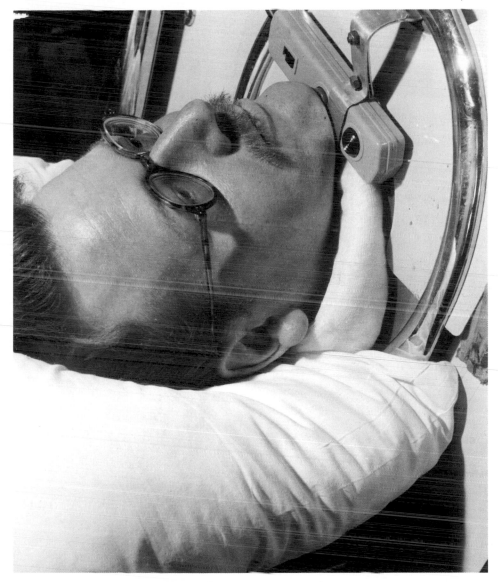

Hi-tech. The great-grandfather of all computers, January 1948. The control desk of the IBM Selective Sequence Electronic Calculator, New York. It was then the world's fastest calculator, one thousand times faster than any other.

High-Tech. Der Urgroßvater aller Computer, Januar 1948. Die Aufnahme zeigt das Steuerpult des IBM Selective Sequence Electronic Calculator in New York. Er war damals der schnellste Rechner der Welt, tausendmal schneller als jeder andere.

Haute technologie. L'arrière-grand-père de tous les ordinateurs, janvier 1948. Le pupitre de commande du calculateur électronique de séquence sélective d'IBM, à New York. C'était alors le calculateur le plus rapide du monde, mille fois plus rapide que tous les autres.

Eye-tech. A soldier
undergoes an eye
examination, 1945.

Okular-Technologie:
Ein Soldat unterzieht
sich im Jahre 1945
einer Augenunter-
suchung.

Autre regard sur une
autre technologie :
un soldat subit
un examen de l'œil,
en 1945.

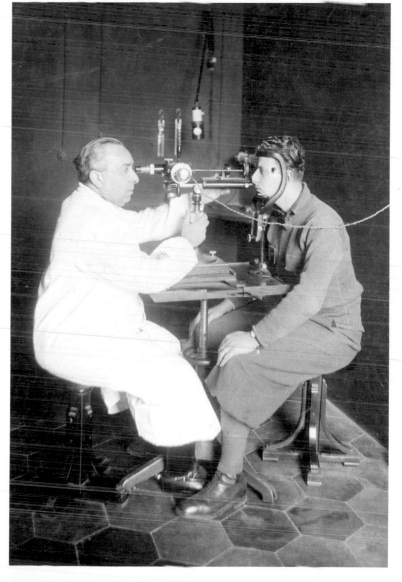

# Index

# How to buy or license a picture from this book

The pictures in this book are drawn from the extensive archives of The Hulton Getty Picture Collection, originally formed in 1947 as the Hulton Press Library. The Collection contains approximately 15 million images, some of which date from the earliest days of photography. It includes original material from leading press agencies – Topical Press, Keystone, Central Press, Fox Photos and General Photographic Agency as well as from *Picture Post*, the *Daily Express* and the *Evening Standard*.

## Picture Licensing Information

To license the pictures listed below please call Getty Images + 44 171 266 2662 or email **info@getty-images.com** your picture selection with the page/reference numbers.

## Hulton Getty Online

All of the pictures listed below and countless others are available via Hulton Getty Online at: **http://www.hultongetty.com**

## Buying a print

For details of how to purchase exhibition-quality prints call The Hulton Getty Picture Gallery + 44 171 376 4525 **(fax)** + 44 171 376 4524 hulton.gallery@getty-images.com

# Acknowledgements

Gerti Deutsch 34, 312
Slava Katamidze 26, 29, 46–7, 52, 89, 136, 172, 200–1, 357